EXPLORING CAREERS IN CHILD CARE SERVICES

By

Jean Ispa

with the assistance of
Elizabeth Vemer and Janis Logan

THE ROSEN PUBLISHING GROUP, Inc.
NEW YORK

Published in 1984, 1986, 1988, 1990 by The Rosen Publishing Group, Inc.
29 East 21st Street, New York, NY 10010

Revised Edition 1990

Library of Congress Cataloging in Publication Data

Ispa, Jean
  Exploring careers in child care services.

  (Exploring careers)
  Includes index.
  Bibliography: p. 133
  Summary: Describes jobs and careers involving child
care, with qualifications for the duties of the job
and suggestions on applying for it. Includes camp
counselors, child development instructors, social workers,
and family therapists.
  1. Child care workers—Vocational guidance. [1. Child
care workers—Vocational guidance. 2. Vocational
guidance] I. Vemer, Elizabeth. II. Logan, Janis.
III. Title. IV. Series: Exploring careers (Rosen
Publishing Group)
HV10.5.I86 1984   362.7'95   83–26851
ISBN 0–8239–1151–9

Manufactured in the United States of America

About the Author

Jean Ispa is an assistant professor in the Department of Child and Family at the University of Missouri–Columbia. She teaches courses describing development during early and middle childhood, methods of working with young children in group care, and methods of working with parents. She also does research on the effects on young children of parent and teacher child-rearing attitudes and behavior.

Dr. Ispa received her doctorate from Cornell University in the field of human development and family studies. The research for her dissertation was completed in the Soviet Union, where she observed young children and teachers in two Moscow day-care centers. After receiving her degree, she worked for three years at High/Scope Educational Research Foundation in Ypsilanti, Michigan. There she conducted research on the social behavior of teachers and children in a mainstreamed preschool (handicapped children integrated with nonhandicapped children), and helped develop and evaluate model preschool curricula.

Prior to graduate school, Dr. Ispa worked as a caregiver for preschool-aged children in a shelter for abused and neglected children in New York City. Her undergraduate major at Cornell University was in social relations, a broad social sciences curriculum. It was after taking a few courses in child development, and after her experience working in the New York shelter, that she decided to pursue a graduate degree in child and family development.

Besides her professional involvement in the fields of child development and early childhood education, Dr. Ispa has considerable personal experience finding and using child-care services for her two children, Simone, age 11, and Zachary, age 7

Contents

Introduction

This book is about jobs and careers that involve one in direct care of children, in teaching others about child care, or both. Day-care teachers, elementary school teachers, nurses, librarians, policemen, and clergymen all work with and for children. In this book, however, we have narrowed our focus to jobs outside of the formal school system that involve either direct care of children on a daily basis or a primary concern with teaching other adults about child care. Caregivers in day-care centers, camp counselors, after-school-care providers, and child health specialists hold such child care positions. Parent educators, high school and college child development instructors, extension agents, social workers, and family therapists hold the kinds of teaching-about-child-care positions we will describe. In the introduction, we discuss some of the advantages and disadvantages of the field as a whole, outline the personal characteristics and values that are most suited to child-oriented careers, and offer some tips for job-hunting and advancement.

Decisions about career choice are among the most important you will make in life. It is good that you are starting to think and read about options now. Having a satisfying career provides much more than money (which is not to underestimate the importance of money!). People who like their jobs derive from them a sense of meaningfulness and fulfillment that is very important to their feelings of self-worth. A job that is interesting and that one is good at adds immeasurably to self-satisfaction and self-confidence. A job is also a source of friends. Holding a job that suits you puts you in touch with people with similar interests and tastes. Many people find that their social lives are much enriched by the acquaintanceships and friendships that begin at work.

The field of child care is in great need of men, and, slowly but surely, more and more men are taking jobs as preschool teachers. It is hoped that this trend will continue; many children derive special benefits from having men care for them. Men who do enter the field report that they, too (not only the children), benefit from its challenges and rewards. We hope that the boys and men who read this book will give child care careers serious consideration.

Since many of the people who choose child care careers are women, a special word must be addressed to them about the importance of having interests and abilities that stretch beyond the home.

Many teenage girls and young women believe that the only route to happiness is through marriage and the rearing of their own children. You may be one of those who believe that immersion in your family will provide you with ultimate satisfaction and security, and for that reason you may invest little thought or preparation in career planning. This is a mistake! Statistics show that in 1980 almost half of all marriages ended in divorce and even in the marriages that lasted, over half of the women were employed outside of the home. Many women whose husbands earn adequate salaries find they simply aren't happy being full-time homemakers. They need to get out and do something else that is interesting and that gives them some of their own money. Women who are single or divorced, or whose husbands' salaries do not permit the life-style they desire, work at least partly because they need the money. You may think that such things "can't happen to me." Many young women feel that way. It is a romantic myth in our society that after Prince Charming comes, you will live happily ever after. Well, "it" *could* happen to you. Many of the women who are employed today harbored the Prince Charming myth when they were younger. Are you *really* so different? Family life is certainly vitally important, but for many of us, professional development is an additional source of pride, challenge, stimulation, human contact, and fun. To be this, it must be nurtured. We are glad that you are starting out by reading books such as this one.

Advantages of Child Care Careers

There are many advantages to choosing a career involving children. The most important one is the sense of fulfillment and satisfaction that comes from watching, supporting, and enhancing children's development. People who work with children *can* and *do* make a difference; knowing that can bring great personal reward.

Second, the need for child care services is increasing as a result of the increase in the number of employed mothers. Jobs *are* available. In 1985, according to the Bureau of Labor Statistics, almost half of all mothers with preschool children and two thirds of those with school-aged children worked outside the home. It was predicted that by the year 2000, 80 percent of all families would have two working parents.

Further, within the general category of child-oriented careers, there are many options. You may enter the profession in one position but later move in other directions as personal goals change. For example, a day-care teacher may, in the future become a preschool administrator, or a consultant to parents. Such mobility is possible and frequently encountered. The knowledge and skills one acquires in one job are not wasted in the next. The parent coordinator, for example, can use her past experience as a day-care teacher very well; teaching gave her insights into child behavior that will help her to understand and deal with the issues that concern parents.

Another advantage to careers working with children is that they never get boring. Every working day brings events that challenge one's skill and intellect. No two days are alike, and there is always something to learn, something to think about. These are not mundane, routine jobs.

When people think about child care jobs, they usually think about interacting with children. That is, of course, a critical and major aspect of work in the field. What people generally do not anticipate is the wide contact with adults that occurs. Many child care workers come into frequent contact with parents, other child care workers, administrators, social workers, and therapists. Some also come to know researchers, school teachers, and a variety of people in other areas that directly or indirectly affect the lives of children. Thus, the opportunity to meet and get to know adults in many walks of life is great.

A characteristic of the child care profession that is not always highlighted but is extremely important is the acceptance by colleagues of the importance of workers' commitments to their own children. Of course, supervisors and co-workers vary in their sensitivity and flexibility, but as a rule it is fair to say that family commitments are understood and accepted more readily by people in this field than in most others. It would be strange if this were not the case.

What does that mean in practice? First, it means that part-time jobs and jobs with flexible hours can be found or created. Preschool teachers and parent educators, for example, often work half-day. Day-care teachers may be able to find a full-time job that permits them to get to work early so that they can leave in time to greet their children when they return home from school. Another possibility for workers that sometimes grows out of colleagues' respect for children and families, as well as from the nature of the work, is that of having their own children in their classroom or in another one in the same building. Some day-care teachers with older children find that their children enjoy coming after school to help entertain the day-care children. Not only does this provide the children with fun and responsibility, but it also solves the working parent's problems concerning after-school care for their children.

Difficulties of Child Care Careers

The advantages of child care careers are easy to acknowledge and make the field attractive to a great many people. It is important, however, for young people considering the field to be aware of its problems. In making your decision, you will have to weigh advantages against disadvantages, thinking all the time about your personal values, goals, and life circumstances.

First of all, let us be clear that you are very unlikely to get rich through a child-oriented career. One of the very real problems of the field is low pay. Child care staff in most programs are paid entirely from parent fees. Especially in their early childbearing years, most parents cannot afford what we believe is the true worth of good child care. In the absence of government financial support of child care programs, beginning day care teachers can expect to earn about $10,000 per year, often with few benefits. Some people do manage to make somewhat more money by serving wealthier families, by opening a private counseling practice, or by going into university research and teaching.

A closely related problem is the relatively low status enjoyed by child care professionals. Many people view child care as requiring no special training or expertise. Nothing could be further from the truth, but the misunderstanding persists. We know a professor who performs a little experiment when he goes on trips. When the person sitting next to him on the airplane asks what he does, he replies that he is a teacher. The response is typically an uninterested "Oh." Then he corrects himself: "Well, actually, what I meant is that I'm a professor of sociology." Now, he says, his companion usually perks up; the "Oh!" is much more interested. This is sad. No one works harder or uses more skills than the good teacher.

The issue of low prestige is currently being actively addressed by professionals in the field. What will it take to change the image? Most people agree that an important step will have been taken when commonly accepted professional job titles are developed and used. The title "baby-sitter," for example, is too often used to refer to teachers of young children, despite the fact that the children are not babies and the adult does everything *but* sit. The results of a recent survey indicate that a substantial number of early childhood workers would prefer titles such as "early childhood teacher," or "early childhood assistant teacher," or "early childhood program director."[1] Other necessary steps for professional upgrading for people who work with children include further development of professional educational requirements and skill standards, rigorous evaluation, and presentation of the situation to the public in a way that increases their awareness and respect. That will take a while, but at least it is beginning to happen.

For some people who attempt child care work, the stress they encounter on the job proves to be too much to handle. One needs a certain amount of inner calm and strength, as well as skill, to deal with people's problems on a close and frequent basis. The child care worker is often confronted not only with children's day-to-day predictable problems (frustration, fighting, boredom, loneliness), but also with parents' needs to talk and get advice and support. This can be very exciting and fulfilling, but it can also produce stress, especially if one feels inadequate to the job. "Burnout" is a term one hears frequently in connection with teaching at any level. A person is said to be "burned out" when he or she loses enthusiasm for work and instead stops caring, performs mechanically and at low energy levels, and even becomes grouchy and brusque with other people. Why does it occur? Researchers have identified several reasons that are applicable to child care and child care training. First is the fact that people may enter the field with high ideals and great personal commitment to "make a difference," and then turn impatient and sour when the realization hits that making a difference takes very hard work and an acceptance of "a little step at a time." Second, many people enter the field inadequately prepared for its demands. Keeping a group of three-year-olds busy and happy takes knowledge and skill. We aren't born with those skills, and they are quite different from the skills

---

[1]Hostetler, L. and Klugman, E. Early childhood job titles: One step toward professional job status. *Young Children*, 1982 (6), *37*, 13–22.

developed by parents and others who take care of children on a one-on-one basis. Third, child care typically involves giving a lot more of oneself than one receives back. Children just are not developmentally ready to understand adults' needs for expressions of appreciation and love, and parents and co-workers also may not think to say "thank you" or tell you what a great job you're doing.

Being closely involved with families is one of the pleasures of working in child care, but it can also be a source of great stress. Through conversations with parents as with children, or by observation, you may become aware of family problems affecting a child's emotional state or behavior. You may even suspect the abuse of a child. Deciding how to intervene can be difficult. In this circumstance you may want to consult a specialist in the area of family counseling for advice and support. A family resource center in your area can be a source of information on this subject.

Most child care facilities have policies to guide you in helping troubled families and children. It is important to be aware of these policies and to know your legal responsibilities. In Missouri, for example, there is a Child Abuse Reporting Law which requires any person with responsibility for the care of children to report suspected abuse to the Missouri Division of Family Services. It is a misdemeanor to fail to do so. The Family Services Association of America or the National Committee for Prevention of Child Abuse, listed in the Appendex, should be able to help you determine the laws and procedures in your state.

Some people who work with children or parents or both all day find that they cannot mentally "leave" their jobs even during their hours off. Their attachment to and concern about the children and families they serve is so great that they cannot just "switch them off." Obviously, important relationships at home can suffer. Moreover, they may be headed for burnout.

Some people find that they are very happy in their jobs until they have their own children. At that point, they find that caring for children at work *and* at home leaves them too drained for either. Some solutions include changing jobs or staying home for a few years, or entering graduate school. The jobs described in

Chapter IX are viable options for persons wanting to make this kind of change.

In the section on advantages of child care careers, we mentioned that one "plus" of the field is the opportunity to meet a wide variety of adults. This is definitely the case, but it must also be realized that these contacts may be brief and occasional unless an effort is made to make them more frequent and meaningful. For example, you may daily see twenty sets of parents, but they may hurriedly drop their children off in the morning and almost as quickly whisk them away in the evening. A good parent program that emphasizes formal and informal parent-teacher contacts can do a lot to make these times more positive and social, and it is important for everyone that this be done. Likewise, social workers and therapists may come and go, doing their work with individual children. The effort should be made to establish communication with these people also, for the benefit of the children as well as of the adults.

The need for stimulation from other adults is naturally great, and another way to get it is through interaction with colleagues. A place where this occurs is at meetings and conferences. That is one reason why attending conferences is so worthwhile; it puts you in touch with others who have the same or similar interests and problems. Conference presentations offer new ideas and insights. People usually find that attending a conference gives them a real boost.

Personal Characteristics for Success in a Child-oriented Field

Just as there is no one perfect mold for children or parents, there is no one mold for the perfect child care worker. Just as there are many different kinds of wonderful children, there are many diffferent kinds of adults who do a wonderful job working with children. There are, however, a few personal characteristics that you should have if you are to work day-in-day-out with groups of children. If you have them, life will be easier for you and the children in your charge. If you don't have them, you may want to consider another field. Not everyone is cut out to be a child care worker!

Here is our list of personal characteristics that fit well with child care:

- First and foremost, a genuine love for children; you must love them even when they are dirty and grouchy.
- Tolerance for ambiguity, for working in a setting where many situations don't have clear right or wrong answers.
- Flexibility. Things don't always go according to plan when you work with children. Sometimes the unanticipated is better than what was planned. For example, you may have planned to tell the children about grasshoppers, but they are more interested in bees or firetrucks. Why not change?
- Ability to think quickly on your feet. Many situations arise daily that require your quick response.
- Tolerance for messes. If you are the kind of person who can't stand messy activities, spots on your clothes, and things being out of place for at least part of the day, you shouldn't be in child care.
- Ability to take things in stride. You should be able to deal with minor crises without becoming unduly upset. People who are fairly easygoing seem best at working with groups of children.
- A positive attitude toward yourself and life in general. Your attitude will deeply influence the group you lead.
- Organization. That may seem contradictory, given the attributes just listed, but it isn't. Children, and adults as well, need schedules, need to know what comes next. They also need to know where things are kept so that they can find them. You shouldn't be the kind of person who can't stand the mess that fingerpainting creates, but you should be the kind of person who sets the fingerpaints out at the right time and then cleans them up at the right time. That way, you and the children will have the security of knowing that there will be enough time to plan and enough time for

the next activity. Children need a predictable schedule; they feel more secure when they have a good idea of what comes next, the flow of the daily routine.

- Ability to work cooperatively with other adults. All child care workers work with other adults: parents, co-teachers, resource persons, students, etc.
- You must be the kind of person who enjoys other people, knows how to communicate with them clearly and supportively, and can face interpersonal problems in a positive way.
- Ability to keep high motivation and effort despite infrequent evaluations. This requires a genuine commitment to children and families. Working with children, you may miss the kind of frequent feedback you get in school. It may happen that for weeks on end no one tells you you're doing a great job, even if you are. Therefore, it is important that you feel rewarded by the job itself, by the progress the children make and the affection they give you. For fairly long stretches of time, this may be the clearest feedback you get.
- Dependability. Parents, children, and your co-workers will rely heavily on you. You must honor commitments, do what you say you'll do, be on time. This is a job that makes you truly *needed*; you must thrive on that and live up to it.
- Good health. Anyone who works with children and families needs stamina. You must be in good health, or it will be very difficult for you to keep up the necessary pace.
- Sense of humor. Without that, you will be frustrated and not have much fun. It's a must!

The chapters that follow describe a number of child-oriented positions in more detail. Each chapter outlines the qualifications and duties of a specific job and gives suggestions as to how to go about applying for it. Read the last chapter for further help in developing a résumé and preparing for interviews.

There is one suggestion that we would like you to consider now, however, even before you go on to read the rest of the book. One of the best things you can do now, while you are considering a career in child care, is to do some volunteer work in a place you imagine to be like one where you would like to work. Many programs for children and parents welcome part-time volunteers. The experience will help you in two ways: it will give you a better idea of whether or not this is really what you want to do for a career, and it will enhance your chances for employment. Employers give a more favorable rating to résumés that show some job-related experience. Many of the supervisors who were interviewed for this book said that they definitely are more impressed by résumés that show that the applicant has had some volunteer experience working with children and parents.

It is encouraging that there is a growing awareness in our country of the importance of childrens' issues, in particular the need for adequate child care. As more legislators are convinced that this is an issue that affects the economy, productivity and well-being of our nation, they are more willing to recognize the need for government financial support for the growth of our child care system. Legislation is being introduced in Congress to try to provide higher quality child care for more American children, and politicians are becoming aware that their positions on child care issues can critically affect the number of votes they get.

Chapter **1**

Baby-sitting: Caring for Children in Their Home

In this chapter we discuss what is commonly called "baby-sitting": taking care of children in their home while their parents are out. The term is extremely misleading, since the job usually entails a lot of everything *but* just sitting (unless the children are asleep), and the children are often older than babies. Another term that is used, although more in England than in the United States, is "nannie." A nannie is a person who cares for children during the day as a full-time, or almost full-time, job. Sometimes she lives with the family. Since no better widely understood terms exist, we shall use "baby-sitter" and "nannie," despite our belief that they suggest less activity and skill than child care actually involves.

Baby-sitting can take a variety of forms and is performed by people of all ages. Teenagers, as well as adults, are often asked by parents of small children to baby-sit for an evening so that the parents can go out. At some professional conferences, baby-sitting services are offered to people who wish to travel to the conference with their children. Many working parents, especially those with infants, prefer to employ a baby-sitter who will come to the home, rather than take their child to a day-care center or family day-care home. These options entail quite different services and quite different levels of intensity of care, but all are called "baby-sitting." We shall start by discussing the kind

1

of baby-sitting that is likely to occur when parents pay someone to stay with their children for a few hours while they go out for the evening.

Many teenagers, young adults, and older people of both sexes have had the experience of being asked to baby-sit for a few hours by parents who want to go out and can't leave their young children alone. What happens when you take this job depends a lot on the number and ages of the children, the time of day, the kind of activities and relationships that the children are already used to, and how well they know you. People who baby-sit say they do it for two basic reasons: first, they like children, and second, it gives them a little extra money. A college student we talked to remarked, "Living in a college community, I never see children or families, just people my age and professors. I miss being with families. Baby-sitting is the only chance I have to be with kids. I love it."

What are some typical evening baby-sitting tasks? Playing with children, comforting them, reading to them, dressing and undressing them, giving baths, changing diapers, feeding, putting children to bed (or reminding them to go to bed), answering the telephone and taking messages. Obviously, this is not all easy, although it should be fun. Some tips that should make the experience more comfortable and enjoyable follow.

First, let's talk about the telephone conversation when parents call to invite you to baby-sit. The conversation will of course be different depending on whether or not you already know each other and whether or not you accept the offer. If you do not know them, they will probably tell you how they got your name and number. You should make a mental note of this and check out the reference. Crimes against baby-sitters are rare, but you should be aware of the possibility. If a friend of yours who knows the family referred you, you can usually feel safe in going to the home. Besides this basic assurance, the friend may be able to tell you some things about the children or parents that will make your evening easier.

If you do accept the offer to baby-sit, be sure to write down the date and time of day you will be expected. Take down the parent's phone number, also. There is nothing so embarrassing for you or aggravating for the parents as your forgetting to come or coming at the wrong time. Remember that they are counting on you. If you have a set fee, you should mention it. Many young people who baby-sit accept whatever the parents want to pay. If that is OK with you, fine. If it isn't, you should be clear about money beforehand. Be sure also to get directions to the home and to arrange for transportation. Especially when they employ teenagers, many parents offer rides both ways. In any case, make sure you know how you're going to get there and back.

If this is your first time with this particular family, plan to arrive ten or fifteen minutes before the parents must leave. There is certain information you should make sure you have, and the children may need a few minutes to look you over while their parents are still there. What information should you have? At the least, you should ask about:

1. Telephone numbers to call in an emergency: the number where parents can be reached, the pediatrician's number, the number for fire or police (911 in most areas), and the numbers of two or three family friends or relatives. Probably you will need none of these, but they may be vital. Put the list of numbers next to a telephone.

2. Rules regarding children's use of television. May they watch any program they choose or only certain programs? Some parents allow children to watch for only a half hour or an hour; others totally prohibit TV watching. Find out the rules in this household.

3. Food and drink. Are you to serve dinner? If so, what will you serve, where it is, what time do the children eat? May the children have snacks? Do they usually have a bedtime snack? If so, what may they have?

4. Instructions about disciplinary techniques, first-aid instructions, or at what time a child needs to be given medication. Such things are extremely important to remember.
5. Bedtime and bedtime rituals. Many families, especially those with small children, adhere fairly strictly to a certain bedtime and a series of bedtime rituals, such as bathing, brushing of teeth, and reading a story before the children go to sleep. Children go to sleep much more easily if their familiar patterns are respected. Find out if lights should be on or off, if a special blanket is needed, and so on.
6. What time the parents plan to be back and, if necessary, how they will get you home.
7. Whether it is all right for you to sleep after the children are asleep? Most parents don't mind if a baby-sitter naps on the sofa, but you should make sure.

Some parents, especially those with very small children, may have a hard time leaving. Much as they have looked forward to the evening out, they also worry about leaving the child with someone new. Will the child suffer? What if a fire starts? Will the baby-sitter have trouble putting the children to bed? These are typical fears that enter parents' heads as they leave the house. Help them! Look confident, smile at them and at the children, help the children say good-bye. Often small children cry when their parents leave but stop a minute or two after the door is closed. You might tell parents this; it will reassure them. Do not suggest that parents sneak out while the child's attention is diverted. This practice subverts children's trust in their parents and makes their lives harder in the long run. Parents *should* say good-bye and, if the child is old enough to understand, explain that they will come back while he is asleep. If a child does cry, redirect his attention to toys or something else interesting.

While the parents are away, it is your responsibility to follow their directions as best you can, to keep the children safe, comfortable, and happy. Play with them, read to them, feed them, bathe them, put them to bed—whatever is appropriate. Be friendly and warm and firm. We have all heard of kids who just won't go to bed with a baby-sitter. With some experience and perhaps some reading on child management skills, you can learn to avoid this predicament.

When the parents return, tell them briefly about your evening. It will make them feel good to hear that things went well. Emphasize the positive, but don't lie. If you had difficulties, you may want to tell them and ask how they handle such situations. Do not criticize the children; phrase the issues that arose in positive or neutral terms. For example, instead of "I couldn't get Johnny to bed on time," you could say, "Johnny was so excited to have someone new to play with, it took him a little longer than usual to settle down to bed." Because parents love their children and feel responsible for their behavior, when you criticize their children, they feel as if you are criticizing them. Be careful. Don't spoil the evening for them unless you have to. If it was too hard an evening for you, you can always find a polite excuse next time they ask you to baby-sit.

Before you leave, the parents should pay you. Remind them if they forget. Many parents will ask what you charge; some will just give you what they think is fair payment. If you have no idea what to charge, it is a good idea to have previously asked your friends what the going rate is.

A growing number of communities are sponsoring short courses for teenagers who baby-sit. The courses are often offered through the public library and cost nothing. Take one if it is available.

Another short-term child care job that some parents offer and that many young people enjoy involves accompanying the family on a vacation. Payment usually includes the trip (travel, lodging, and meals) and some cash. You take care of the children when parents want time to themselves; typically, you also get some free time of your own. Thus, you might entertain the children while the parents ski or go to a concert, but you have time off in the late afternoon. You probably won't make a lot of money doing this, but you will get a free trip and a lot of fun. Look for parents seeking vacation child care in newspaper classified ads and in high school and university bulletin boards and placement services.

Would you like an extended stay abroad? Write to the U.S. Department of State and to the American Embassy in each of the countries you would like to visit and offer your child care services. Many American diplomatic families with young children hire live-in nannies. Payment may be airfare, room and board, and some pocket money. You may also be referred to native families who would like someone to care for their children and teach them English. We know of young people who have thus earned themselves trips to countries all over the world, including the Soviet Union. Explained one young woman who accepted such a job, "How else could I have gotten to live in the heart of Paris? I care for a six-year-old boy twenty hours a week, and the rest of the time I'm free to explore. Sometimes I take him with me: he's my excuse to visit the circus, children's theater performances, and so on."

Let us now turn to a related but different job—regular (usually daytime) child care in the child's home while the parents work. People who perform this service call themselves by various titles: baby-sitters, child care providers, nannies. It is often a full-time job but it can also be done part time.

The people who take these positions represent quite a diverse group. Many are women with no higher education who enjoy children and do not want the menial jobs they might otherwise get. Many are new immigrants to the United States who have limited employment possibilities because they have not gone through our educational system. Quite a few are people pursuing a university degree; this part-time job helps pay tuition and living expenses. Some are college graduates who prefer this type of work to others, but this is not typical.

What kind of work is involved? The same kind as the evening baby-sitter's but with more intensity and, probably, some light housework (washing dishes, vacuuming, perhaps preparing meals and doing the laundry).

Many families employ a nanny *and* a person who cleans, so that your responsibilities are limited to child care. That, of course, is preferable to a job where you have to do everything. As for child care, you can expect to be kept busy playing with the children, taking them on walks, comforting, feeding, diapering, toilet training, singing, reading, and whatever else the children need and the family expects.

You will truly be a substitute parent, and if all goes well you and the children will develop warm bonds of affection. You and the parents will also develop affection for one another. Parents tend to become very attached to the people who regularly or frequently come to their home to provide child care. "I just love her," said one mother. "She takes such good care of Ben, and it's wonderful to have someone to talk to who knows him almost as well as I do. I rely on her completely. It scares me to death to think she might quit someday. I *need* her!" There aren't many jobs that can give you such a feeling of being loved!

Where does one go to find such positions? The classified ads of almost every newspaper are good places to look. Look under "Baby-sitting," "Instruction," and "Child care." Often jobs are found through word-of-mouth. University placement offices post parents' notices.

When you learn of a potential position, call to arrange for an interview. When you call, give your name, state that you are interested in caring for children and ask if the position is still open. If it is, it is appropriate to ask about hours, salary, number and ages of children, and location. If these are satisfactory to you, say that you would like to arrange for an interview in the home. You will want to meet the family and find out more about the responsibilities involved, and the parents will want to talk to you to see if you "fill the bill." Go prepared with references— the names and telephone numbers of people who know you well, preferably people for whom or with whom you have worked.

You will make a good impression if you show interest in and warmth toward the children and respect and friendliness toward the parents. The interview is the time to give evidence of your honesty, sincerity, responsibility, and warmth. It is also the time for you to ask questions and get as clear a picture as possible of the job requirements and of how you feel about the family. You don't want any disappointing surprises.

Some metropolitan areas have training programs for nannies, or live-in child care workers. Programs such as Nanny, Inc. in Chicago and the National Academy of Nannies in Denver offer training in child care theory and practice. Topics such as activities to promote numbers and reading skills, nutrition, safety, family relationships, and even cardiopulmonary resuscitation are included. The demand for graduates of these schools is high, and the pay is good. At this writing, nannies can earn $800 to $1,500 per month plus room and board and, sometimes, use of the family car. Families who can afford such nannies are, of course, well off themselves, so there are likely to be extra benefits such as living in safe neighborhoods and having access to various amenities. At present, there are few schools for nannies, but the number is likely to increase. For information, write:

American Council of Nanny Schools
Delta College
University Center, MI 48710

Chapter II

Early Childhood Center Teacher or Aide

A center-based program for teaching and caring for infants and young children is one that is housed in a classroom-like setting in a building that is not someone's home.

Many centers are housed in buildings built specifically for child care. These usually have three or more classrooms, each with fifteen to twenty children and two teachers. Many other centers are housed in renovated single-family homes, store fronts, or elementary schools. Almost any kind of building can be made into a day-care center. Day-care centers housed in church basements are common. Many churches rent or donate their Sunday School facilities for this purpose during the week. A growing number of hospitals and businesses are finding that employee morale is raised and absenteeism and even turnover are reduced by the availability of day care at or near the work-place.[1] Thus, day-care facilities can be found in some progressive factories, hospitals, and office buildings. The Employee Benefit Research Institute reports that the number of employers offering child care assistance (referrals or actual care) tripled between 1982 and 1985 alone. As more women with children enter the work force and become valuable employees, this number should continue to grow.

---

[1] Women's Bureau. *Community Solutions for Child Care.* Washington, D.C.: National Manpower Institute, 1979.

It takes a lot of skill and energy to keep a group of children happy and interested.

Center-based child care programs go under a variety of names and espouse a variety of purposes and philosophies. Some are called nursery schools, some preschools, some day-care centers, and some day schools. Other terms such as early childhood center are also used. In reality, however, what the center is called tells little about its goals or its method of operation. The only certainty is that programs called day care are open eight to ten hours a day and provide care for children while their parents work. The other terms are used both by half-day and full-day programs.

For persons working directly with children in child care centers, there are basically two possible job titles: head teacher and assistant teacher (sometimes called teacher aide). Many preschool classrooms have one head teacher and one assistant teacher, although in some centers there are no such distinctions; all are teachers with equal status.

Aides, or assistant teachers, usually (but not always) have less education and fewer years of relevant experience than head teachers. Their salaries are somewhat lower, and they carry less responsibility for planning activities. In many cases they nonetheless spend just as much time with the children as the head teacher and are just as important to the children. In some centers, part of the aide's job is to free the head teacher of routine tasks such as setting up activities or meals, cleaning up, and taking the roll. Training is often on-the-job. That is a good way to get experience. It is common for aides to move into head teaching positions as they become available.

For more information about either of these positions, write to the National Association for the Education of Young Children. The address is given in the Appendix. This association sponsors national and local conferences, publishes excellent books and brochures about early childhood education, and presses for high standards and rights for children and the professionals who serve them.

American Child Care Services operates the Child Care Personnel Clearing House, which distributes information on summer and full-time child care jobs for students and recent graduates. Their publication, *Help Kids*, lists jobs. Write to American Child Care Services at the address listed in the Appendix.

Another organization that might prove helpful if you are considering becoming a teacher aide is:

Student National Education Association
1201 16th Street, NW
Washington, DC 20036

One of the most basic decisions you must make if you decide to work in a child care center is the age group you want to work with. While center-based care is less common for infants and toddlers than for 2- to 3-year-olds, the number of such facilities is growing. Infants and toddlers are usually cared for in groups of four to eight. Ther ratio of caregivers to children varies from center to center; different states have different standards for licensing purposes. Thus, you may find centers where caregivers must work with more infants or toddlers than state regulations recommend.

Some recent research has shown that infants in full time day care may have problems with insecurity.[1] These findings have caused concern about the wisdom of placing those under a year in child care centers. It is sad that mothers who return to work and who have managed to find infant care must also worry about possible harm to their babies because of their choices. It is likely, however, that the quality of the center and care giver are important in determining whether or not a child does well. Things to notice about a center, other than the ratio, are the physical environment (is it clean, pleasant and stimulating?), the quality of interaction (do staff members respond, quickly and warmly to a child's needs?), and whether developmental needs of infants are being met.

Programs that provide infant care usually do so on a full-day basis. The center is likely to be open from about 7:30 a.m. to 6:00 p.m. Each full-time caregiver works an eight-hour day, so that the one who arrives at 7:30 a.m. leaves at 3:30. Shifts are staggered so that enough caregivers are available at any time of day. Thus in the same center there may be a 7:30 a.m.–3:30 p.m. shift, a 9:00 a.m.–5:00 p.m. shift, and a 10:00 a.m.–6:00 p.m. shift. There are also likely to be part-time jobs in day-care centers, often at the after-school times of 3:00 to 6:00. If you are considering a career in the care of young children, it may be fruitful for you to apply for such a position. If no paid positions are available, consider offering your services as a volunteer.

What personal qualities does it take to work with infants and toddlers? In the Introduction we listed some that apply to all child care professionals, and later in this chapter we add some that apply specifically to work with 3- to 5-year-old children. For work with infants and toddlers, we must underline the need for warmth, enjoyment of cuddling and a lot of close body

[1]Belsky, J. and Rovine, M. (1988). Nonmaternal care in the first year of life and the security of infant-parent attachment. *Child Development*, No. 1, 156-167.

contact with babies, lack of squeamishness (there will be plenty of dirty diapers, spit-up, and runny noses), patience, strong nerves (for those times when three babies are crying but you only have two arms, or when you have to get back from your walk but the toddlers are dawdling and can't be rushed). Also extremely important is the ability to relate to parents in a sensitive, confident manner. Parents of very young children are often unsure of themselves and need a lot of support. Many also feel guilty about not staying with their little ones twenty-four hours a day and need to be reassured that their children are getting good care and not suffering.

Since babies' schedules are not as predictable as older children's, schedules in infant day-care centers have to allow for flexibility. Over the course of a day, a caregiver can expect to be engaged in playing with and talking to children, feeding, changing diapers, rocking, soothing, taking children on walks, giving medication to those who need it, and talking to parents. Keep in mind that this is very different from baby-sitting for children for a few hours while their parents go out for the evening. For one, there will be several infants or toddlers, not just one, as in most families. Second, you will be responsible for their welfare for whole days at a time, not just for a few hours once or twice a week.

Part-day programs for 2½- to 5-year-olds typically enroll children for three hours a day. They are usually attended by children whose mothers are at home all day but believe their children need some group experiences to gain independence and learn to get along with other children and adults. Full-day programs usually entail a morning of planned and unplanned activities, then lunch and naptime, followed by free play until parents come to take their children home.

There are many philosophies of early childhood education. Before you begin looking for work, you should be familiar with the most common models (traditional nursery school, open-framework, Montessori, didactic, etc.) and know which one you want to adopt. All work with children requires patience, kindness, and creativity, but some programs also require religious teaching, or a very structured approach, or a very loose approach, or make some other demands that you should believe in and be comfortable with if you are to be happy and do a good job.

Since the passage of PL 94-142 (the Education for all Handicapped Children Act), an increasing number of preschools are enrolling handicapped children along with nonhandicapped children. If you are to be working with handicapped children, you must learn some of the techniques of special education. You can do this through reading, talking to therapists and special educators, or taking college courses.

Let us outline a typical day for a day-care teacher of twenty 3- and 4-year-olds:

7:00-7:30	Arive at work and start getting the room ready for children. Set out some activities (paint, clay, etc.).
7:30-9:00	Greet children and parents as they arrive. Help children get involved in free play.
9:00-9:30	Breakfast and brush teeth.
9:30-9:45	Group time. Gather children in a circle to discuss the day's events, read a story, sing, play a record.
9:45-11:30	Free play or planned activities indoors and outdoors (there is great variation here from center to center).
11:30-11:45	Help children clean up after their activities.
11:45-12:00	Read to children.
12:00-12:45	Lunch and brush teeth.
12:45-1:00	Put down cots while children look at books quietly.
1:00-2:45	Children sleep.
2:45-3:30	Children awake; snack is served. The teachers who came in at 7 a.m. go home at 3:00.
3:30-6:00	Planned and unplanned activities. Greet parents as they arrive to pick up their children.

Part-day programs are usually open from about 8:30 to 11:30 a.m. and from 1:00 to 4:00 p.m. The program may be similar to the morning activities of a full-day program except that breakfast and lunch are not served; the snack may instead be served at midmorning. Of course, exact schedules vary in detail from program to program, but the one illustrated above will give you an idea of a typical day.

What kind of person finds working in an early childhood center with 2½- to 5-year-olds satisfying? What kind of person is especially good at it? Refer back to the Introduction to our list of personal characteristics that are found in successful early childhood teachers, and add these:

- A firm belief that early childhood is a critical period in human development.
- A desire to be directly involved in supporting and guiding the development of young children.
- The ability to derive satisfaction from small accomplishments.
- A feeling of personal satisfaction from the knowledge that one has contributed toward giving some children a good start in life. Commitment deep enough to carry on despite relatively low pay and social prestige.
- Openness to new ideas. You and the children in your care will have a much better time if you continue to seek and try out new ideas for activities and methods of relating to people.
- The ability to plan for and manage groups of young children as well as individual children.
- An understanding of how to break large tasks into smaller, more manageable ones.
- Acceptance of different kinds of people. Racism, sexism, prejudice toward the handicapped, the poor, the foreign-born—in short, any kind of negative attitude will hurt you and them. You must be capable of accepting and showing interest in a wide variety of people.

The ability to work cooperatively with other adults is critical. This teacher enhances home-school relationships by inviting parents in to share their trades.

- An honest awareness of one's own weaknesses and a willingness to compensate for them in positive ways.
- Leadership qualities. You will be guiding children, parents, and other professionals. You will need the self-confidence and ability to do this.
- Expressiveness. If you are a shy, inhibited person, you may have trouble contacting the children, role-playing with them, singing with them, sharing in their joys and sorrows. People who are not afraid to "act like a kid" are probably best suited to work in early childhood education. You should be comfortable recognizing and bringing out the child in yourself.
- Acceptance of the fact that you will have to do a lot of clean-up work. Most centers employ a janitor, but teachers and aides are nevertheless responsible for keeping rooms neat and counters and table tops clean.

Maintaining a safe, secure, and stimulating environment for a group of lively young children takes a great deal of understanding and skill. Many people underestimate the complexity of the task. A young man we know who is taking college courses in early childhood education invited his friends to come and observe him "in action." Later, he told us that his friends were impressed. "They used to tease me that I was preparing to be a baby-sitter. Now they have a lot of respect for what I'm doing and realize how much training it takes. Watching me with the kids made them think again."

Where does one get the kind of training one needs to be an effective early childhood educator? Many people currently in the field have had little or no formal training. This is unfortunate, since research has indicated that day-care children do best when cared for by teachers who as students majored in child-related fields.[2] Some high schools provide courses and practicum experiences that are good introductions to the area. Our experience, however, is that the most comprehensive and in-depth training is that available in most colleges and universities in departments of child development, human development, or education. Coursework in such departments covers various essential areas of knowledge and skill: normal stages of child development, the development of handicapped children, family processes, assessment procedures, activities and group management skills for work with young children, understanding and communicating with parents, and administration of early childhood programs. A college major in a child-related field typically requires attendance at lecture courses, participation in seminars and workshops, and involvement in a practicum placement in an early childhood program.

Another option is to obtain a Child Development Associate (CDA) credential. This is a credential usually awarded to child care workers who have not completed a bachelor's program in

---

[2]From the findings of the National Day Care Study, conducted by Abt Associates, Cambridge, Massachusetts, 1978.

early childhood education but who have had considerable on-the-job experience and have put together a portfolio of materials showing their understanding of and ability to implement strategies for work with children in thirteen functional areas (safety, physical development, language, and so on). The credential is awarded after the candidate's portfolio has been accepted as competent and complete and after positive evaluations of his or her performance by a trainer, a parent-community representative, and a consortium representative. If you are interested in this on-the-job training program, write to the following address for an information booklet and application form:

Council for Early Childhood Professional Recognition
1341 G Street, NW
Washington, DC 20005

The Child Development Associate credential is recognized nationally; it gives you professional mobility since it travels with you.

If, for some reason, you are not in a position to get either college or CDA training, try to get a job in a center that offers its own in-service training. Head Start is one such program. Head Start staff members participate in career development training programs that include monthly workshops and feedback from education coordinators.

Remember that at this writing there is no required across-the-board certification or license for working with young children in day-care centers. Many centers do, however, give preference in hiring to persons who can demonstrate that they have had some solid professional education in the field. Also, programs sponsored by public school systems hire only graduates of college early childhood education curricula. We strongly believe that you will be a more effective teacher and that you will have more fun if you come to the job with the appropriate professional education. Some states do require some type of certification or licensing for early childhood positions. You can check with your local chapter of the Association for the Education of Young Children for specifics regarding your state.

How can you find out about the quality of the center to which you are applying? One way, of course, is to ask people who have been there. Another is to observe on your own. A third way is to find out which centers have qualified for voluntary accreditation, which is sponsored by the National Academy of Early Childhood Programs. For information about accreditation, write to the Academy at 1834 Connecticut Avenue, NW, Washington, DC 20009-5786.

What are some of the advantages of working in a child care center? Again, the Introduction outlines the positive aspects of child care careers in general. In our interviews with center-based early childhood teachers, we heard over and over again that "We're important; we make a difference." This seems to be the primary attraction of the field: early childhood teachers know that their work really matters, that what they do makes a real impact on children and families.

Other teachers talked of enjoying the daily opportunities for creativity, the autonomy they felt they had, the variety of people and experiences built into the job, and the fact that the job is demanding but usually not super-stressful. Some also mentioned that their own children are cared for at the center at reduced rates, and one teacher noted that she values the job security. The demand for child care is so great in our country that one can almost always find and keep a job or become a family day-care provider in one's own home.

What are the difficulties of this profession? As mentioned in the Introduction, the major complaint is about salaries. They are low, and opportunities for advancement within a center are usually limited. Advancing typically means going into administration, and administrative work is mostly office work, away from the children. Indeed, we know of people who have tried administrative work, missed having a lot of direct contact with children, and gone back to classroom teaching despite a resulting cut in pay.

When asked about job frustrations, one preschool teacher

said, "The hard part is the wet pants, the dirty faces, parents wanting to know why their children are so dirty. Sometimes I also wish I could get dressed up once in a while to go to work, but I know that'd be the day I'd get paint on myself." If looking "just so" is important to you, this is not the job for you!

Another issue raised by several teachers concerns the lack of feedback. As one teacher put it, "You may know you're giving it your best shot, but you don't *really* know what impact it had. You must have deep inner conviction about what you're doing and be rewarded by the belief that you're helping a small number of people. I used to want to change the world, make the whole world a better place to live. Now I understand how unrealistic that was. I just hope I'm making these children's lives better. They don't thank me. I just have to believe it."

For many people, the advantages of the profession outweigh the disadvantages. For some, work in a child care center is a step on a career ladder that later takes them elsewhere. Talk to a group of high school or university child development teachers or professors, psychologists, elementary school teachers, and therapists, and you will find quite a few who worked as early childhood educators early in their careers. A common pattern is to hold such a job for two or three years after graduation from college, then to go on for a master's degree in a related area. It is a good path to follow because it gives you a wealth of practical experience and knowledge upon which to build later work.

How does one go about getting a job in an early childhood center? Many teachers reported that they had simply answered newspaper ads or job notices posted on college bulletin boards. Others looked in the Yellow Pages and called every school, then followed up by sending a résumé to the directors of the centers that had openings. Some used their informal networks to find out about job openings.

Your résumé should show your educational background. If you have taken child-related or family-related courses, list them specifically. If you majored in early childhood education or child development, be sure to indicate it (you needn't list each individual course). Clearly show all relevant jobs you have had, whether paid or volunteer. Finally, list the telephone numbers and addresses of people who can serve as references for you.

When you go for an interview, be prepared to share your philosophy of preschool education—your goals for children and parents, the kind of structure or atmosphere you believe in, the schedule you'd like to follow. The match between your philosophy and the center's is extremely important. In some centers, you may also be asked to teach for a few hours so that the staff can see how you actually work with children. Refer to Chapter XI for more specific tips regarding job-hunting, résumé-writing, and interviewing.

This student enjoys baby-sitting because it's her only opportunity to be with children.

Chapter III

Family Day-care Providers

In Chapter II we gave you an overview of what it is like to work with young children in an early childhood center. This chapter is about providing care for a smaller group of children in your own home. There are many similarities between the two options, but also some important differences. Let's look at the similarities first:

- Most family day-care providers work with a *group* of children.
- Family day-care providers should have the same love for children and the same kinds of child management and stimulation skills as the center teacher.
- Ability to communicate comfortably and completely with parents is important.
- Social prestige and income are usually relatively low (although income may be higher than that of center teachers).

While the similarities between the work of a center teacher and a family day-care provider are fairly obvious and certainly important, the differences are also significant. Let us start with the *relative advantages* of taking care of children in your home, as compared with taking care of them in a center:

- You are independent, your own boss. You are the teacher and the director. You have no supervisor.
- You can care for your own children as part of your work. Most family day-care providers have small children of their own. Taking care of a few other children as well often makes it financially possible for them to stay home with their own.
- You may enroll just one or two children if you wish, or a larger group if you wish. (Check your state licensing regulations for the maximum permitted.)
- The care you provide will probably be more familylike, and many parents prefer this for their children, especially for infants and toddlers.
- You may enroll children of varied ages, for example, an infant, a couple of toddlers, a couple of preschoolers, and a couple of school-aged children who come after school. Having a mixed-age group can definitely work to your advantage.
- You may be able to do some of your household chores even while you work. For example, you can cook your family dinner while children play; if you have a small group, you can even take them grocery shopping.
- One family day-care provider told us that an advantage for her was that through her work she has learned a lot about activities for children and that this has made her a better and more involved mother. "If I didn't have the other children here, I'd probably just sit and sew all day. This way I'm more actively involved even with my children."
- Your children will always have playmates right at hand.
- One can earn more money as a family day-care provider than as a center teacher. The income itself may be higher. Moreover, you can take income-tax deductions for your yard, the parts of the house you use for child care, toys, and even your car if you use it for field trips. Thus, to figure out how much money you make, you should add parent fees

and money saved from income tax, then subtract expenses. Income-tax deductions are particularly helpful if you are married and your spouse earns money that would otherwise be heavily taxed. Your job then provides a tax shelter for you both.

- Finally, because you have a smaller group of children, you may get to know them, and particularly their parents, better than you would in a larger center.

These advantages make family day-care attractive to many people. Those who choose to provide it are usually women with small children or an entrepreneurial spirit, or both. Also important, according to several women whom we interviewed, is a husband who supports the idea and doesn't mind pitching in once in a while. "It takes a certain kind of man," said one, "to feel O.K. coming home to find other people's kids still here, parents coming in and out, toys around, and so forth."

This brings us to the *relative disadvantages* of providing care in your own home, as opposed to in a center. Here are some points to consider:

- Your house may be more cluttered and your furniture gets more wear and tear than otherwise.
- Your work days will probably be longer. It is unlikely that you'll work an even eight-hour shift. If one child comes from 7 a.m. to 4:30 p.m. and another child from 8:30 a.m. to 6:00 p.m., you will be on duty from 7 a.m. to 6 p.m., an eleven-hour day. Some caregivers we know sleep with the children at naptime so that they can make it through the day.
- You will have to be the teacher, the cook, the dishwasher, the janitor, the accountant—in short, there will be no division of labor; you will do it all.
- Your income may fluctuate unpredictably as children drop out, parents don't pay on time, and so on.

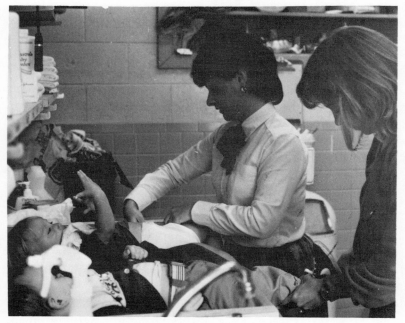

Infant care means diapers. In a day-care center two can do it simultaneously.

- You may feel isolated if you have no adult contacts most of the day. That can lead to loneliness and a feeling of being stuck.
- As mentioned above, it may bother your spouse to come home to extra children, parents collecting their children, and a clutter of toys.
- Your own children may find it too hard to share their parent, their home, and their toys with other children. In fact, many family day-care providers send their own children to preschool or to another family day-care home because of this problem. In that case, of course, one of the advantages of family day care, having your own children with you, is lost.
- The parents of the children you care for depend on you completely. Although you shouldn't, you may feel quite

guilty taking a vacation, or you may feel terrible about calling parents to tell them you are sick and can't work. Many family day-care providers solve this dilemma by agreeing to serve as backup for each other. Thus, if one is sick, another will care for her children until she recovers.

The daily routine of family day-care providers varies from home to home. Nevertheless, we will describe a schedule that shows a reasonable and fairly typical series of events in a day-care home.

7:00-8:30	Greet parents and children as they arrive. Have quiet activities available for children. Prepare and serve breakfast.
8:30-10:00	Get out activities for children. Interact with them as they play.
10:00-10:30	Prepare and serve snack, probably with children's help.
10:30-11:30	Outdoor play.
11:30-12:00	Engage children in preparing and serving lunch.
12:00-12:45	Eat and clean up.
12:45-1:00	Read children a story, prepare sleeping area.
1:00-3:00	Children nap. Caregiver naps too or takes care of chores.
3:00-3:30	Children awake and snack is served. School-aged children may arrive.
3:30-5:30	Supervision of children's play. Greeting of parents as they arrive to pick up their children.

There are no formal educational requirements for family day-care providers, although persons with some background in early childhood education and child development will probably find the work easier and more satisfying.

Most states have voluntary licensing programs for day-care homes. Licenses are awarded to providers whose homes meet certain health and safety requirements and whose groups of children are not too large (six children per adult is a typical maximum). In some states the provider must also have some training in child development and nutrition. Missouri licensing regulations, for example, require that the provider show proof of having:

— adequate indoor and outdoor play space for the children;
— a daily schedule of planned activities, such as art time, story time;
— adequate equipment to maintain and develop children's health, safety, and mental growth;
— nutritious weekly menus of two snacks and one lunch per day;
— fair admission and discharge policies;
— medical reports on the children signed by their physicians;
— proof of provider's health and a negative tuberculosis test;
— forms requesting parental consent for field trips;
— parents' instructions in case of emergencies.

A list of licensed homes is maintained by the licensing agency and provided to interested parents. The fact that a home is licensed may also be reassuring to parents who are trying to find good care for the children while they work. For those reasons, licensing may help the provider in recruiting children. Being licensed is also beneficial because it gives the provider herself the sense that she is at least keeping to some standards set forth by professionals as minimally adequate. Of course, it is hoped that the care provided will more than surpass the minimal standards.

Also find out if there is an established formal or informal network of family day-care providers in your area. Recognizing the importance of family day care in the United States, a growing number of communities are developing networks of caregivers. These networks function as support systems. There may be meetings and workshops sponsored by social service agencies or university extension programs. Most family day-care providers find such networks very helpful and supportive.

How do you establish yourself as a family day-care provider?

First, if you wish to be licensed, and we hope you do, contact the appropriate agency in your area to ask for the regulations. If you don't know where to call, look at the listings under your state (e.g., "Virginia, State of") in the telephone directory and call the agency that appears to handle services to families and children. The person who answers should know with whom to connect you. You might also call a local preschool to find out this number; any preschool director should know.

We also suggest that you get in touch with your local Association for the Education of Young Children (AEYC). You can write to the National Association for the Education of Young Children for the name and address of a local member. You will find that reading AEYC materials and attending meetings are excellent ways to get useful information and to find people who understand what you are doing because they are doing it too. Indeed, several day-care providers mentioned to us that this is one of the best ways they know to fight burnout.

The next step will be to plan your program and possibly to buy equipment and toys. You will have to think about menus and grocery shopping, about a daily routine you'd like to follow, and about the number and ages of children you'd like to care for.

You'll have to plan a budget, figuring out expenses and what you will charge for care. Some policy decisions must be made. Will you ask parents to pay for days when their children don't come because of illness or vacations? Should parents be required to keep a complete change of clothing for their child at your home? May children bring their own toys? Will you buy extra cribs and high chairs or will you ask parents to supply them? Will children have the run of your house or will they spend most of the time in one area, a family room, for example?

You will probably have to buy some toys and equipment. Buying them new will immediately put a serious crimp in your budget, so garage sales and other sources of used items can be extremely helpful. Just get there early; good used equipment goes fast!

You should become familiar with a variety of activities that appeal to and benefit children. Activities and materials should be available that challenge children's minds, provide opportunities for positive social interaction with peers and adults, and facilitate their language, creativity, and physical development. Keep in mind also that bored children are likely to become naughty children. The Bibliography will help you find books with ideas for activities.

Another important set of decisions concerns discipline. You must decide how to handle discipline among the children in your care. The books in the Bibliography can be of great help in this respect, too. They describe the use of positive language, redirection, behavior modification, and other techniques that promote positive behavior in children. Once you have children in your home, try to find out how each parent handles misbehavior. It may be hard for a child to make the transition between two different sets of rules and disciplinary strategies. At least in the beginning, you may have to approach the issue in a way similar to the parents' way.

Once you have your house ready and have decided how many children you want to take in, and at what ages, you are ready to start recruiting. As time goes on and you become established and develop a good reputation, you may be able to fill openings simply by word-of-mouth referral (one parent telling others). In the beginning, however, you will probably have to put an ad in the paper. Your classified ad should indicate the ages of children you want, your hours, your fees, your location, and your phone number. Some successful providers add something like "loving care, nutritious snacks and lunch," as selling points. In some areas, you can also post notices on bulletin boards in supermarkets and other public places.

When parents call, invite them to come to meet you and your family. When they come, show interest in their child and answer all questions as honestly and completely as you can. Tell them about your policies regarding fees, vacations, illness, and so on. Tell them about yourself and your family and about the kind of care you will provide. The first interview is crucial. First, it is the only grounds parents have for deciding between you and another provider they may be considering. Second, if you do care for their child, you will in fact be inviting him or her to join your family, and you will be seeing the parents almost every day. You want to start on a friendly footing, with as much mutual understanding as possible.

Some experienced family day-care providers suggest that you also find out as much as you can about the family that has come to interview you. Because the relationship between a family day-care provider and the families she serves is so close, it is easiest if you feel good about them and agree with their child-rearing philosophy. One provider told us, "If the parents don't really love their child, I don't want to get involved. It's because I get so attached to the children, I can't stand it if I feel they're suffering. Then I feel too sorry for the child and feel down. I don't want to feel that bad." Other family day-care providers, on the other hand, said that they want to help those children who don't get enough love from their parents. It is for you to decide how you want to function.

Once you and a group of parents have decided to have their children come to your home for day care, you will have to set a starting day and ask parents to bring some supplies and some information. You may also want to invite them to stay with their child for the first hour or so, to help him or her adjust to you and the new setting. Sometimes a short visit the day before is equally helpful.

What should you ask them to bring? Here are some suggestions:

- A paper giving the child's name and birthdate, allergies or other medical problems, each parent's full name and work telephone number, physician's name and telephone number, and any other pertinent information you would like to have.
- A complete change of clothes for the child.

- A favorite blanket, stuffed toy, or other "lovey" the child likes for security or napping.
- Appropriate clothes for outdoor play.
- Diapers, formula, baby food, if needed. (Most child care providers do not supply infant formula or baby food even though they supply lunches for older children.)

Like all child care professions, providing family day care is demanding but rewarding. It is different from some of the others because it actually involves owning and operating a small business. A challenge indeed!

Chapter IV

After-school Care

As more and more mothers are entering the work force, there is a rapidly developing need for good-quality day care and after-school care for older children. With large numbers of school-aged children of employed parents needing a safe and stimulating environment, both after school and during summer vacations, career opportunities are expanding in this field.

Many communities now recognize the needs of school-aged children and their parents. Although limited facilities for elementary school children have existed since the 1940's, it is only since 1970 that after-school programs have grown rapidly in number. All indicators point to after-school care becoming a field that will employ many new child care workers and professionals.

As you think about a career working in an after-school program for children, you will want to consider the different models that are currently being used in many communities. These have been developed on the basis of children's needs, parents' expectations, and community resources. Basically, there are three types of programs, which are categorized by the facility in which the program operates: (1) school-based programs, (2) center-based programs, and (3) family-based programs. Each type has both advantages and disadvantages and provides distinctly different work environments for the child care worker. We will expand on this later in the chapter.

When you think about working in an after school-program, what do you expect it to be like? The U.S. Office of Child Development describes the goals of school-age day care as follows:

> It should care for and protect children, it should reinforce a child's ethnic and cultural heritage while allowing him to become an integral member of society, it should supplement both home and school, it should foster the development of a sense of self-worth and confidence and the ability to function independently in the environment, it should make him aware of various life-styles and promote respect for individual differences, it should stimulate his cognitive and sensory abilities, it should teach him to work productively with youth and adults and also to work alone, it should help him to work and carry out plans, and it should teach him responsibility for his words and actions.

Those are certainly appropriate goals for school-aged children, and they represent a real challenge to you as you work with them. However, you will find that the way the goals are met, or how a particular program is designed, depends upon the available facilities and equipment and the knowledge and experience of the adults working in the program. Therefore, you, as a child care worker or after-school-care professional, will need to select carefully the program that best meets your qualifications and career goals.

The Office of Child Development Survey and numerous after-school-care administrators all state that the primary objective of after-school care is to provide a safe and well-supervised environment for children after school. Some centers also offer services to children before school, providing transportation from the center to the school. The next priority is an excellent activity and recreational program for children who have been involved in a busy and structured classroom setting all day.

Some centers also provide tutorial programs to help children with their schoolwork. Additionally, you will find programs that allow parents to bring ill children to the center so that the parents will not have to miss work. You can see that after-school care is both similar to and uniquely different from many occupations in which you work with children.

Advantages of Working in After-school Care

For anyone considering a child-centered career, volunteering in an after-school program is a good way to try out your skills, as well as help you decide if you're interested in the field as a career. After-school programs offer flexibility in scheduling: before school, after school, and, in some centers, during the evening and night as many centers accommodate parents in varying work schedules.

Working with children in an after-school program will contribute to the development of your skills in interpersonal relations as you work with the children, their parents, and other staff. One head teacher told us that this training is invaluable, as you need to be constantly attuned to the children's feelings, and you gain skill in both listening and problem-solving. She added, "You also must be willing to apologize, as children of this age are very sensitive and don't always understand adults' humorous attempts to alleviate a stressful situation." But the rewards are great, as you can see results through changes in behavior. You gain a real sense of how you can affect individual children.

Another professional, who administers the after-school program at one of the 700 Kinder-Care centers, said, "I love working with the children, they are exciting!" She described her work as never dull and having many rewards as the children really respond to challenging, creative, and innovative programming efforts. Since children of this age enjoy games and imaginative play, the creative adult can develop his or her own skills and knowledge of children by working with them in a setting very different from that of the elementary school.

Disadvantages of Working in After-school Care

All the professional after-school-care people we interviewed cited low salaries as the primary disadvantage in the field. This is, at the moment, not a high-salaried profession. In some centers, a person with or without a bachelor's degree receives a salary at or slightly above the minimum wage. However, there is room for advancement, as people with administrative skills move up to develop programs and curriculum and manage community and statewide programs. One director of a private program said she declined professional advancement because it would take her away from the children, and working directly with children was her personal reason for choosing the field. Another head teacher in an after-school program cited personal initiative as a factor in obtaining a salary increase. She said, "You have to tell your supervisor. Document how you are doing more, and that you now need more salary."

Another disadvantage that many workers in this field cited is the relatively low public image of the after-school-care worker, the lack of professional respect by the general public. A professional administrator said, "I resent people regarding me as a baby-sitter; I have a Master's Degree in Child Development, teach children, counsel parents, and manage the business and fiscal affairs of this center."

Some centers that offer programs for school-aged children are hampered by lack of facilities and equipment, which puts constraints on the extent of the activities that can be offered. Many community and private centers primarily serve preschoolers, and the after-school program is an adjunct to the preschool care. Therefore, the equipment and facility design may not be appropriate for school-aged children, who may resent being associated with a "baby school." Also, many school-based programs, although convenient, have severe restrictions on both space and equipment utilization, so that the staff of the after-school program has to be innovative with ideas and activities to make it successful for the children.

Reading to children is an important part of the day-care teacher's job.

Other teachers have described after-school care as rewarding, but also very stressful. In an after-school program, the teacher-pupil ratio is much larger than in preschool. The children come from school where they have accumulated the day's stressors, hurts, and fatigue. The after-school caregiver needs to be attuned to each child's needs. The high demands of others and little opportunity to be alone or talk with other adults can contribute to professional burnout.

All career choices have advantages and disadvantages as well as myths and realities. In choosing a career that will be rewarding and satisfying to you, you need to examine all aspects and options in the field. Talk to workers and professionals about their jobs; think about volunteering so that you can see for yourself what the myths and realities are. Child care careers are rewarding, exciting, and challenging. They also can be stressful, underpaid, and misunderstood. It is a good idea to think about and find out about these aspects of your choice before making your decision to work in and with an after-school-care program.

Job Specifications and Responsibilities

The following job descriptions will give you general information about some of the careers open to you in the after-school-care profession. The job titles may vary from community to community, but the educational requirements and job responsibilities will be similar.

Program Director

The After-school Program Director develops cooperative agreements with community agencies and organizations that can provide programs for different ages and interests. This person also supervises special programs and activities of the after-school coordinators and manages sometimes complex transportation schedules.

A program director must have experience in the administration and supervision of a child-oriented program. Minimum educational requirements are a bachelor's degree in education, psychology, or a related field. The salary depends on experience, the size of the program, and the funding source. Usually three to five years of experience in an administrative capacity is required. You also will need strong managerial skills in business operations and personnel management.

After-school Program Coordinator

The After-school Program Coordinator works in one school or agency. Coordinators identify participants in the program through working with teachers, counselors, parents, the juvenile justice system, and students. Additionally, you will develop each child's weekly activity schedule and perhaps help the children with their schoolwork through the center's tutoring program.

You will also recruit volunteers to work in the special-interest areas of the program.

You must have at least two years of college coursework pertinent to working with children and adolescents. A college degree is preferred. You will need job experience in working with children. Volunteer work and experience such as summer camp work would be good references. Several employers we talked to indicated that they gave preference to applicants whose educational background was in education or parks and recreation. Knowledge of school-age children is a must. Salaries range from the minimum wage to slightly above, with the possibility of advancement with increased education and experience.

School Day-care Coordinator—School-based

In this position, you are assigned to an elementary or a junior high school, where you enroll children in the program. You also work with the administrative staff in scheduling activities and supervising program aides.

The educational requirements are at least a high school diploma, and some college is preferred. Most employers also look for an applicant who has a work history in programs for children and youth and also supervisory experience. Organizational skills are very useful, and excellent communication skills are essential.

After-school Program Aide

You will primarily supervise the children enrolled in the program. However, you may also assist in tutoring and recreational activities.

Most communities do not have formal educational requirements, but they often prefer that program aides be residents of the community they work in. Again, good interpersonal skills and some experience with elementary and junior high children

Guiding without interfering — the balance good teachers must strike.

are helpful. This is a good place to try out your skills and see if you would like to continue to work in this field.

School-age Day-care Coordinator— Family Day-care Services

Some communities have developed school-age day care that is provided in homes by family day-care providers. These services care for children who are ill or whose parents work evening or night shifts, offer after-school care, and serve children with special needs who are best served in a home setting.

The coordinator is an information and referral base for parents and family care providers of school-age services. You will be the liaison between parents, licensed care providers, schools, and social service agencies who need child care services.

High school is the minimum educational requirement, and most communities require at least one year of experience working in community programs. A successful applicant also must have tact, discretion, and good managerial skills and be able to work with minimal supervision.

Family Day-care Provider

Many school-aged children receive after-school care from licensed family day-care providers. In most cases, this is a home that is licensed to provide care for preschoolers as well. It is described in detail in Chapter III.

Job-hunting Tips

Employers will be interested in your educational background, your volunteer experience, and your paid work history. Of equal importance are your personal attributes and skills in working with children and adults. In any career in which you work with children, you need flexibility and patience. You also should be willing "to do a lot of things," as in these programs you will have varied and sometimes unpredictable duties. Good health and a high level of energy are essential. A sense of humor is a definite asset, for both you and the children you work with. An administrator of an after-school program at a large university emphasized that after-school-care personnel really benefit from ongoing training in the needs of school-aged children. She also suggested that assertiveness training was very useful in working with this age group.

When applying for a job, you should check your community resources for school-based programs. Most communities also have private centers as well as family day-care centers. Your educational background is an important factor as you enter the job market. Child development, psychology, education, or parks and recreation are good majors for people who want to work with children.

As we talked with administrators of child care programs, they indicated that their most valuable college courses were those in which they got practical training by working directly with children in their child development labs. Reading about children is necessary and helpful, but you also need "hands-on" experience.

Additionally, those working in this field said they really should have included business courses during their college training. Many aspects of their jobs were concerned with business practices: bookkeeping, staff recruitment, training and evaluation, budgeting, and recordkeeping. They recommended that people going into the field seek out coursework in business and management as an adjunct to their training in working with children.

In many communities the after-school-care program is in daily operation, including weekends, holidays, nights, and summer vacations. Therefore, job opportunities are frequently available on either a part-time or full-time basis. This is a field that is rapidly developing in many communities.

Detailed information on after-school care can be obtained by writing to the School-Age Child Care Project, Wellesley College Center for Research on Women, Wellesley College, Wellesley, MA 02181.

Chapter V

Summer Camp

Whether you are a high school student or a graduate with professional training, summer camps are places where you can work with children and other adults in a beautiful outdoor setting. As a staff member of a summer camp, you will have opportunities for both personal development and professional growth. You will not only improve your job-related skills, but you will also develop your interpersonal skills as you work with both children and other adults. This can lead to future jobs in your area of interest or in related fields. Many of the skills you develop will transfer to other professional disciplines and life areas.

In resident camps, or "sleep-over" camps, children spend the night, as well as the day, for a week or more. Children attending day camps return home every evening. This chapter focuses mostly on resident camps; there is a section on day camps at the end.

When you begin looking for a resident summer camp you would like to work in, you will find that there are many variations in quality and size. However, the American Camping Association (ACA) has accredited more than 2,000 camps in the United States, and a camp that meets the association standards has met qualifications in 300 areas covering its facilities, programming, and staff development.

What is a good summer camp like? First of all, it is a child-centered community where the staff has total responsibility for the well-being of the campers. The environment provides support for both campers and staff as the camp experience develops understanding of self, others, and the community. The goals of a good camp program focus on developing children's knowledge and appreciation of the natural environment as well as providing experiences in which each child can achieve success and acceptance with others of different backgrounds and interests. The ACA has defined the purpose of a camp program as "... a sustained experience which provides a creative educational opportunity in group living in the out-of-doors. It utilizes trained leadership and the resources of natural surroundings to contribute to each camper's mental, social, and emotional growth."

Those goals are accomplished in many different settings. Have you ever wanted to live in the mountains? Live in another state? How about spending your summer at a beautiful northern lake? A summer camp can take you anywhere!

Programs for campers are as varied as the locations of camps, but all are organized on the basis of the total growth and well-being of children. You may choose a camp that offers skill development in a physical area of your interest such as tennis, horsemanship, basketball, or other sports. You may want to consider a program that concentrates on the fine arts, with eight- to twelve-week programs of individual and group instruction in art, music, or dance. A number of camps offer programs for children with special problems: cerebral palsy, hearing impairment, diabetes, emotional trauma. However, most camps offer a variety of programs so that children may be exposed to and experience many areas: outdoor activities, interpersonal relationships, enhancement of self-esteem, and specialized skills.

Advantages of Working in Summer Camp

We have already mentioned many advantages of work in a summer camp. Since jobs are available all over the United States, you may choose the part of the country in which you would like to work. If you want to spend the summer in a beautiful outdoor setting, a resident camp is a good place to do so.

Even quiet projects are more fun in the summer sun.

Additionally, as you investigate camps, you will find that they serve children from elementary school age to high school. In many cases, you may choose the age of children you most enjoy working with.

If you want a job that is stimulating, challenging, and different each day, you will find it as a camp staff member. A good camp program encourages its staff members to use their own creativity in working with the children, allowing them an opportunity to develop their own strengths.

Working in a summer camp can be a work experience during your high school years, a year-round career with some of the larger camps, or a combined vacation–learning experience from your primary job. Many teachers choose to work in summer camps; it is therefore not age-limited, nor necessarily only a summer job.

Your work with the campers can be extremely gratifying, as you have the potential of helping children learn and grow in their camp experience. You will be the recipient of hugs, kisses,

Residential care may look much like day care.

and tears as you share some very special experiences with the children.

Perhaps the most important advantage to the camp staff member, as regards future career, is the development of interpersonal skills in working with others. Your contacts with other staff in many related fields can be invaluable, both during the camp season and later on. You will form many friendships as well as future career contacts.

Disadvantages of Working in Summer Camp

Children are wonderful and children are interesting, but children can be demanding, physically and emotionally, when you have twenty-four-hour responsibility for their care. When you are a camp counselor, it is much like parenting, as you have little free time. Most camp personnel report that being aware of this, keeping healthy and rested, having knowledge of children, and above all keeping your sense of humor, will help you enjoy this responsibility.

Another disadvantage is that the salaries for most camp positions are lower than some other jobs for which you may be qualified. However, that is offset to some extent as most camps provide you with food, lodging, laundry services, and health care. Many staff members also view a summer camp experience as a combined vacation and job. If your goal is to make a large amount of money during the summer, however, this probably won't be your choice.

For some people a major disadvantage of a resident camp is that one's social life and work life are primarily in the same place. This works well for many people but is difficult for others.

Since summer camps offer many skill areas, serve many child populations, and are located in all areas of the United States, opportunities are available for anyone choosing a career working with children. Before making your decision to work in a camp, what do you need to consider? One camp director with fifty summer employees said:

"One of the biggest considerations staff need to decide in accepting a camp job is the decision to live in a camp *community* ... a community where there is a lot of give and take, sharing, and adjusting to others, both campers and staff. The residential aspect of the camp setting leaves little free time for self. Social needs of staff are met by full commitment to joining in with everyone who lives in the very special camp community for twelve weeks. Only by joining in with 100 percent enthusiasm for the job and mission of the camp will staff find real satisfaction."

A Typical Day at Camp

The wake-up bell rings about 7 a.m., followed by breakfast, announcements, and group singing. In many camps the children are given responsibilities for cabin cleanup, flag-raising ceremonies, group entertainment, and so on. After this, cabin groups begin their planned activities for the day. There are usually three one-hour activities in the morning and two in the afternoon. Activities may be swimming, hiking, rock-climbing, creative movement, outdoor skills, or maybe working on a play or program for evening campfire. A good camp provides precamp training as well as trained specialists to work with you and your group. You may have planned an overnight campout with your group, or perhaps an out-of-camp canoe or bicycle trip.

By noon it's time for lunch, and then a one-hour siesta. Both campers and staff benefit from this quiet time to rest, read, or write letters. Afternoons are usually at a slower pace than mornings. At four there is a block of free-time when the children may choose their own activities with supervision.

After dinner comes another quiet time before the evening program, which is a highlight of the day for campers and staff. Responsibilities for evening programs are shared among various cabin groups. This is another opportunity to use your creativity as you plan and complete the group activity with the children. After the campfire and songs the campers' day ends with lights out by 9 to 9:30.

After the campers are asleep, relief counselors supervise the cabins and the camp staff meets to evaluate the day's program: its strengths, difficulties, and ways to improve. This is an important part of the day for staff, as it is a time to socialize with peers and share your concerns, enthusiasm, problems, and frustrations. It is an important part of the support system for staff. As you share your experiences with others, you receive both support for and feedback from your efforts.

Since good health and energy are essential for staff as well as campers, you will probably be in bed by 10:30 or 11 p.m. Camps do not allow staff to leave camp during sessions, except for days off. Days are long; it may be very hot, cold, or rainy, and your enthusiasm, planning, and sense of humor are the catalysts for the children's well-being and enjoyment. The day sometimes goes smoothly, but you will have occasions when your best planning goes awry, and your flexibility, energy, sense of humor, and sensitivity to the children will determine whether it's a successful experience. You will work with homesick children, those with illness, blisters, bee stings, and poison ivy. Some children have fears of snakes, water, and nightmares. Life at camp is not predictable, and the camp staff is the crucial element in the children's adjustment.

You may choose the geographical locale of your camp, the age of the children you want to work with, and the skill you are developing. However, there are personal considerations such as your stamina, flexibility, personality, psychological attributes, and job-related skills and training that will ultimately influence your job decision. The following career options, with their job descriptions, qualifications, and responsibilities, will help you to assess your needs with the descriptors specified by many summer camps. More detailed descriptions follow later.

Camp Staff Positions

Position	Minimum Age	Minimum Educational Requirements
Program aide	16	High school student
Junior arts and crafts instructor	18	High school graduate
Junior pool instructor	18	Current Red Cross WSI
Cabin counselor	18	High school, some college preferred
Campcraft director	20	College student
Creative arts director	20	Teaching experience
Nature director	20	Junior in college or more
Pool director	21	Current Red Cross WSI
Resident employment skills counselor	22	College graduate, or more
Unit director	21	Junior year in college, or more
Senior arts and crafts instructor	21	Two or more years of college
Child guidance specialist	—	Master's degree, counseling
Trip director	21	College degree, or more
Administrators	25	Bachelor's or master's degree, 3–5 years' experience

Program Aide

This position offers mature qualified teens with a strong interest in children an opportunity to develop their skills in interpersonal relationships in a group setting. You will have a "hands-on" experience that will develop your knowledge of working with children. You will also receive future job references as you accumulate a work history in many areas of camp operations.

Qualifications: Applicant must be sixteen, and in high school. Emotional maturity and the ability to work effectively with campers and staff are essential. Additionally, you must be in good health, have enthusiasm and a positive attitude, and enjoy outdoor living. You also need some recreational skills.

Responsibilities: You will assist the counselors, program staff, and camp administration. Specific duties might include assisting at the pool, nature activities, crafts, overnights, and cookouts. You also will help counselors with special activities and act as a relief counselor. Above all, you will be a model for the campers.

Pool or Waterfront Director

This position requires skill in giving group swimming lessons, noting safety hazards and correcting them, delegating responsibilities to helpers, and maintaining the pool or waterfront.

Qualifications: A senior instructor must be twenty-one, a junior instructor, eighteen. Both are required to have current Red Cross water safety instructor certification.

Responsibilities: You must have the ability to run a safe, healthy, and stimulating program. Responsibilities are delineated by each camp, but you will be expected to supervise all operations of the swimming program and usually take complete charge of pool maintenance.

Arts and Crafts Instructor

This can be a really exciting job if you are aware of the possibilities for artistic and individual expression that an arts and crafts program allows. You need experience in a variety of media and must be able to incorporate the use of found and natural objects into the activities.

Qualifications: A senior instructor must be twenty-one with two years of college; a junior instructor should be eighteen. Both should have experience in teaching arts and crafts. Also important are the ability to work with staff and children and to do advance planning and organization.

Responsibilities: You will supervise all operations of the program, developing activities that are appropriate and challenging to campers' various stages of development. You will also provide training for, and coordinate efforts with, the counselors.

Cabin Counselor

As a cabin counselor you are responsible for the health, safety, and emotional well-being of your group. If you would like to work directly with children and can work effectively with other counselors and staff, this position can be very satisfying. Doug Z., a counselor said, "You folks showed me a kind of fellowship and commitment to others that I've never seen before. I think the only thing more beautiful than the kids we worked with was the dedication to those kids by the people around me. I feel as though I grew more in the past twelve weeks than in the previous twenty-one years."

Qualifications: Most camps require a minimum age of eighteen but may prefer some college. You should have the ability to relate positively to your group of campers. As in all camp jobs, you need emotional maturity, energy, good health, and an appreciation and understanding of children.

Responsibilities: You will assume round-the-clock responsibility for your group. A cabin counselor is sensitive to the needs of individual children and is a friend to the campers while maintaining adult status. Additionally, you will be trained in camp skills, which you will teach to the campers. If you have a sense of responsibility, mature judgment, leadership qualities, and ability to accept supervision and to work with children without harshness, you and your campers can look for a rewarding camping season.

Campcraft Director

You will teach basic camping health and sanitation standards, conservation rules, and camping etiquette with the philosophy of having minimum impact on the environment.

Qualifications: Applicants should be at least twenty and have at least some college training. Most camps also look for experience or skills in teaching, camping, scouting, or related outdoor activities. You also should have some skills in leadership methods and techniques.

Responsibilities: You will supervise all operations of the campcraft program and develop activities that are appropriate and challenging to campers of different developmental stages.

Creative Arts Director

This position varies according to the goals of camps but entails planning activities in which the children can explore their creativity and imagination through movement, performance, or dramatic play.

Qualifications: You should be at least twenty and have some teaching experience. You need knowledge of the benefits children gain from participation in creative experiences. Sensitivity, creativity, and knowledge of children are essential.

Responsibilities: You will design the creative arts program and involve the children and staff in it. In many camps, this program is the fastest growing one, as the children show great enthusiasm.

Nature Director

The nature director plays an instrumental role in helping

campers discover the wonders of nature and overcome any fears they may have: of insects, water, snakes, storms.

Qualifications: Most camps require you to be at least twenty, with three or more years of college training. Your course work should be in environmental education, biology, or other related sciences. You also need the ability to carry out and coordinate a comprehensive nature program.

Responsibilities: Your goal will be to involve campers in the process of learning, appreciating, and respecting the natural environment.

Resident Employment Skills Director

Supervisory positions in a summer camp setting are available if you have advanced training and experience in specialized skill areas. Camp Wyman in Eureka, Missouri, is piloting a Resident Employment Skills Program designed to teach job skills in conjunction with a recreational camp experience, thus helping teens to facilitate their transition to the job market.

Qualifications: Applicants must be college graduates, have at least two years' experience as a supervisor, and have skills in planning, organization, and management. Experience in junior high career exploration is also helpful.

Responsibilities: You will have many responsibilities, including training and working with camp administrators and supervisors and designing and teaching seminar classes. The RESP director coordinates and schedules work experiences and maintains volunteer networks and outside resources.

Unit Director

This is a multidimensional leadership job that requires excellent organizational and managerial skills. The unit director plays many roles: administrator, recreational leader, counselor, friend, teacher, and mother/father figure.

Qualifications: Applicants must be at least twenty-one, with three or more years of college and one or more years of supervisory experience. Many employers look for extracurricular activities and volunteer service. Skills in organization, planning, and management are also helpful.

Responsibilities: You will plan creative and well-structured programs for children and provide leadership in decision-making. You will also work in a one-on-one relationship with campers and other counselors, make evaluations of counselors, and review counselors' daily schedules.

Trip Director

This position requires technical skills, leadership and supervisory experience, confidence, and a positive attitude. Being a trip director is an interesting, challenging job that offers opportunities for personal and professional growth. You will be responsible for training campers for successful out-of-camp experiences and overnight activities such as canoeing, hiking, and bicycling.

Qualifications: Applicants must be at least twenty-one years of age and college graduates. Also needed are technical skills in specific areas such as canoeing, cycling, rock-climbing, as well as the ability to work positively with the campers.

Responsibilities: The specifics vary among camps, but all require persons with a high degree of maturity, responsibility, motivation for fulfilling camp goals, and ability to make good decisions.

Child Guidance Specialist

This position, available at some camps, is open to one who has the professional knowledge and skills to evaluate camp programs and the staff's role with children.

Qualifications: A master's degree in child development, counseling, or a related field and at least three years of teaching or guidance counseling experience. Emotional maturity, good health, and the ability to work effectively with other staff are important considerations.

Responsibilities: You will develop effective strategies for the camp counselors to use with the children to insure that the camp environment is a positive and relaxed emotional climate for both children and staff. You will work with staff in behavior management and in-service training and teach positive discipline skills to counselors.

Administrative Positions

Administrative personnel are professionally trained in specific areas. The camp director usually has at least an undergraduate degree and extensive experience in interpersonal, organizational, managerial, and fiscal areas. The director is responsible for the success of the camp in meeting its goals through the development of the program and the selection and supervision of a large group of employees. Other professionals are often involved in the development of programs designed to meet the needs of the particular population the camp serves. The administrative staff also serves as a liaison between the camp and the community and plans and implements precamp and ongoing training programs for staff.

Day Camps

Day camp programs are operated by cities, youth organizations, churches, and individuals. They vary in the quality of programs, and you will want to evaluate several camps before making a decision.

Many of the qualifications and responsibilities of the staff positions are similar to those for a residential summer camp, but there are some differences. In a day camp you may work with younger children, aged 6 to 10. You may not have as many facilities as a resident camp, and frequently you may develop more of the program yourself. Usually the groups of campers are larger, and you have a somewhat different relationship with the individual children, as you are with them only six to seven hours a day, five days a week.

Advantages of Day Camp

You will have evenings and weekends free for your own activities, which may be appealing to you. You also may stay in your home community if you choose. The situation is one in which you gain experience working with both adults and children in an outdoor environment, but it is not as demanding as the twenty-four-hour responsibility of the summer camp.

Disadvantages of Day Camp

To some degree, the shorter time spent with the children, as well as the larger group size, may be disadvantageous. Many counselers view the intense involvement of summer camp as a very positive experience in which you gain a great deal of knowledge of both children and adults. This is usually not possible in a day camp.

Programs may be more limited, you may have fewer specialists to work with, and you may have less of a sense of community with the children and staff. Salaries also tend to be rather low, with many jobs paying the minimum wage. However, there is great variety among day camps, and you may need to do some research to find the one that fits your needs and qualifications.

JOB-HUNTING TIPS

Careers in resident camps for children offer many options for summer employment or a full-time vocation. Some job descriptions specify educational requirements and technical or professional skills. However, thousands of job openings in camps occur each year where the core qualifications are a knowledge of child development and a strong motivation to work with children in a natural environment. If you have the qualifications and enthusiasm a camp is looking for, they will provide an excellent training program in which you will be able to develop the specific skills you need for the camp program. Through a camp experience, you will develop numerous skills that are applicable to your personal and professional growth.

Salaries range from $400 to $1,500 for the summer season and include food, lodging, and health care.

When you have your interview with a prospective camp employer, he/she will not only be interested in your educational accomplishments, volunteer activities, extracurricular interests, hobbies and skills, but will also evaluate your personal attributes. The employer is interested in a candidate who portrays:

— a positive attitude toward self;
— a positive attitude toward children;
— warmth, sincerity, flexibility;
— tolerance for stress and pressure;
— energy.

You will be asked to submit a résumé and references. Most employers ask job applicants questions similar to the following:

How will this job provide you with personal growth and development?

How do you maintain good communication with children and other adults?

How would you handle a problem situation with a supervisor?

What do you think would be the strongest contribution you could make to our camp?

What motivates you to apply for this job?

Camps begin to interview for summer positions in February or March. Interviews are frequently held on college campuses or can be arranged by contacting the individual camps. You may find camp advertisements in the back pages of young adult magazines, newspaper listings, and your career guidance office. However, a comprehensive list of over 2,000 accredited camps may be found in:

The Parent's Guide to Accredited Camps
American Camping Association
5000 State Road, 67 N.
Martinsville, IN 46151

An organization of camp owners and directors is:

National Camping Association
353 West 56th Street
New York, NY 10019

Chapter VI

Group Home Care

Residential facilities, or group homes, provide both short-term and long-term care for children and adolescents. These facilities offer career opportunities for persons who have a high school diploma, an associate degree, a bachelor's degree, or postgraduate training. In a unique setting, a residential counselor functions somewhat like a parent, responding to the children's emotional and physical needs in a homelike environment. In many facilities it is a 24-hour-a-day responsibility.

In a residential setting, the children usually have special needs: children who have developmental delays or disabilities, children who are awaiting placement in foster care or in adoptive homes, or adolescents who are in need of a structured environment provided through community resources or the juvenile justice system. Thus there is a wide variety of facilities from which to choose, and they serve children of varying ages and many different needs. Group homes are located in both rural and urban settings throughout the United States.

Although residential counseling often entails assuming the role of "houseparent," it is both similar to and different from the parenting role. First, what are the similarities to being a parent? You will be a nurturant figure and a role model for your group of children. You will also be responsible for meeting many of their emotional and physical needs. That may mean comforting a child when he or she is having a nightmare, shopping for jeans and running shoes, and perhaps taking a child to a dental appointment. You will work with children on their social skills:

You will not only play with them, but also teach them to improve their group interaction and their interpersonal skills. That may be accomplished through structured activities or shared events such as movies, pizza parties, and school functions. In many residential homes you will also teach the children practical skills as well as train them in personal care.

How is being a residential counselor different from being a parent? First of all, you will be a member of a team of professionals. As such, you will be responsible not only for meeting the children's needs, but also for implementing your team's plan for accomplishing goals for the children in your care. Those goals may be specific behavior changes, improved social skills, increased individual competencies, or improved self-care abilities. You will have a great deal of autonomy in implementing individual programs, but you will also have supervision and support from other staff members.

In many group homes you live in the home with the children on rotating shifts. Some homes have a five-day work schedule (24 hours) and five days off; others schedule employees on a two-week work period with the two following weeks free. In some group homes you work an eight-hour day, and relief counselors are available for the evening and night hours.

The job outlook in this field is excellent, as there is an increasing trend toward deinstitutionalization in most situations where children and adolescents have special needs. There is also a shortage of quality foster-home care for children. Additionally, most teens do better in a group home with peer support than they do in many foster homes. During the next decades, we expect to see more families realizing the advantages of group home living, with its increased independence, for their developmentally disabled children.

Advantages of Working in a Group Home

When you work with children in a residential setting, you are working in a natural setting. You not only deal with the children's stresses and problems, but you work with them, laugh with them, share with them, and even may cook dinner with them. You are able to reach them in a different way through daily interaction. Several counselors cited this aspect of residential counseling as a real plus for the job. You really know the children.

This job is an excellent way, perhaps one of the best ways, to get an overall view and understanding of people and their problems. You will have opportunities to work with the whole person, using social work, counseling, and teaching skills. It is a good way to define your interests. It is also an excellent way to discover if you really want to work in a helping profession.

For many people, the flexible scheduling offered to staff in group homes is a distinct advantage. Since many residents of group homes are at school or at work during the day, most staff jobs begin after school. Therefore it is a good way for college students to have a comfortable place to live and gain valuable work experience. The scheduling in blocks of time worked followed by blocks of time off is also cited by many counselors as a distinct advantage. With this flexible scheduling, you may plan trips and vacations more frequently than you can when you have only weekends free.

One counselor stressed that the work is exciting. You are involved in and are a part of the children's lives. You share their joy, pain, struggles, and successes. The work is not routine, and for many it is both challenging and exciting.

Disadvantages of Working in a Group Home

Some counselors told us that they received low salaries for very demanding work. However, others felt that salaries in the field are improving, and they cited the fringe benefits of room or apartment, meals, telephone, and utilities, which made the salary competitive with other helping professions.

For some people, the hours of work are seen as a disadvantage. Many group home staff members work evenings and weekends. However, most supervisors try to rotate staff and suggest that employees trade shifts so that no one always works on Friday and Saturday. Staff members work on some holidays and are required to respond to some emergency calls even when off duty. Even though this is not a predictable 8-to-5 profession, many people find the schedule works well with their individual biorhythm.

As in many of the helping and child care professions, group home staff members frequently describe their work as emotionally draining. The intense interaction may contribute to the rather high burnout rate in the profession. One staff member told us that you become so involved that you may find it hard to remember to keep supporting other staff members. We'll talk more about the ways some counselors deal with these issues later in the chapter.

A social worker we interviewed, who had worked in a group home for adolescent girls, described the social isolation of her job as a major disadvantage: Your home and your work are in the same place. Also some residential homes are situated in isolated country settings. You may want to consider these factors as you think about career choices.

In some group homes job descriptions may be rather vague. Some people view this as an opportunity, whereas others may see it as a disadvantage in that tasks and authority are not always clearly delineated. You may want to ask questions about this during your job interview.

Personality Attributes

People who do well working in a group home are those who can consistently set their own limits and boundaries. They are able to convey to others their expectation that their privacy is to be respected. These people are able to be fully involved in the moment with the children, but they are also able to *enjoy* their own recreation. In essence, those who do well in this profession are those who are able to define whose problems are whose. The job is a good way to learn that.

Those who find real satisfaction in this job are people who

enjoy people. A counselor we interviewed explained that the most successful in this work are those who enjoy doing things with, not for, people. She suggested that a good psychology student may not necessarily be good in such a setting. The job requires someone who is able to flow with the situation, not someone who feels the need to control the situation.

Flexibility is a crucial factor in group work that may have little correlation with college degrees. Flexibility also includes a respect for individuals and for individual differences.

One counselor described the importance of sensitivity and empathy, or the ability to imagine yourself in another's place. Many who work in group homes have had personal experiences that have helped them. One very effective staff member in a group home for the hearing-impaired was the child of deaf parents. Another counselor said that a number of good counselors are "used to being in a grocery store and having people stare at you."

Everyone we interviewed who had worked in a residential setting mentioned a sense of humor as being essential in the profession. You will need this sense of humor both to get and to keep your perspective in many situations daily.

A staff supervisor we interviewed told us that her most successful staff members had many of the above qualities. One was a physical education teacher, another an accountant, and a third a biology student. They all shared the quality of respect for people and their individual differences. They also were able to share laughter and warmth with the children in their care.

Job-hunting Tips

Your personal qualifications and your volunteer experiences are very helpful as you apply for a job in this field. Volunteer experience during your junior high and high school years are excellent preparation for work in a group home. You will find many group homes, summer camps, and other programs for children that need volunteers to help implement their programs.

Your local newspaper and personal visits to these facilities are good ways to find volunteer opportunities to try out your skills.

As we said earlier, a college degree is helpful but not required for group home counselors and child care workers. All group home workers do need a solid knowledge of normal human development. Many group home supervisors suggested that people who are interested in this area of the helping profession design their college coursework around their specific area of interest; i.e., rehabilitation psychology, developmental disabilities, adolescence, child development, and social work. One administrator explained that you also need many practical skills, such as basic nutrition and how to grocery shop to provide nutritious yet economical meals and snacks.

When you are looking for a job in a group home, you may consult your local newspaper. However, the best way to find the job that fits you is to go to the places in which you would be interested in working. Talk to the staff, interview them, and leave your résumé. They will contact you when they have an opening. When an employee leaves, he or she gives only two weeks' notice. Those who already have their applications on file will be the first considered for the job opening.

When you go for a job interview, most employers will present to you several problem situations and ask how you would resolve them. The problems are frequently situations that have recently occurred in that particular setting. Often there is more than one solution and more than one way to handle a problem. By asking questions and posing problems to you, the interviewer is able to see how you would approach and resolve a given situation.

As a potential employee, you may be asked to attend an orientation program. At one group home, this consisted of attending two dinners and two activities at the home. You also may be asked to spend some time with at least two other staff members. One supervisor explained that potential employees need to talk with at least two staff members in order to have an accurate perception of what the position entails.

Many employers are looking for people who are able to work effectively with little supervision and without a lot of support. Although co-workers do support one another, you will function best in this work if you have your own built-in reward system.

Work in a group home is an occupation with many rewards and satisfactions as you make your own unique contributions to the personal growth of others. The opportunities are available in all areas of the United States in diverse areas of human services for children and adolescents. Working in a group home or residential care may be a rewarding career, or it may be an excellent in-depth training ground for you as you define the area of human services in which you choose to work.

Chapter **VII**

Program Director

The need for preschool and day-care personnel is rapidly expanding. Within the next twenty years more than 20,000 professionals per year will be needed to keep up with the increasing demand for their skills. Within this expanding field of programs for young children, there is an administrator for each program. Opportunities now exist, and will continue to grow, both in established early childhood centers and for those who wish to establish their own preschool or day-care centers.

There is an urgent need for quality care for infants and toddlers as well as for preschool children. In some areas corporations are responding to their employees' needs by developing on-site care facilities for children. This trend is expected to grow, and qualified and concerned professionals will be needed to staff the centers.

The administrator, or program director, of an early childhood program is an important person. The quality of the center reflects the philosphy and the capabilities of the director. Professionally, you will have many responsibilities; however, you will also have many rewards and opportunities.

You may ask, what is administration? One definition is that administration (or management) is the entire group of processes through which human and material resources are made available and effective in order to accomplish the purposes of the project. To be an effective administrator, you need experience, education, organizational skills, and the ability to work with people so

Interviewing job applicants is an important part of the director's responsibilities.

that you can create an environment in which each child and each staff member can function to full potential. All administration begins by defining the purpose and goals of the program. Therefore, you will want to think about your own goals and philosophy of children and families as you consider this career choice; it will help you decide not only on your career choice, but also on your college and coursework.

The minimum educational requirement for most administrative positions is a bachelor's degree in child development or early childhood education. In larger programs, such as corporate day care, a master's degree is preferred. A large part of your job as an administrator is concerned with managerial functions. People who are working in the field strongly recommend that you take coursework in business areas in addition to your child development degree program. In many centers you will be responsible for budgeting, recordkeeping, staff recruitment, training, and evaluation as well as the overall planning, coordination, and supervision of the program.

What does an administrator or program director do? First of all, he or she is engaged in the planning, implementation, and supervision of the program and staff of the children's center. That entails developing a curriculum, material resources, and the recruitment, training, and supervision of a qualified staff. Additionally, you will enroll children, work with parents, manage the budget, and be a liaison between the staff and the board of directors. These basic tasks are fitted into a broad spectrum of responsibilities and daily decision-making. One director cited the many organizational and managerial functions of the director, but she also said that support of the teaching staff was a critical element in the director's job. Another said that a director must be able to walk into the center and sense the flow of activities. She or he must be attuned to who does what in the best way and must organize the center accordingly. The program director also should be able to step in where needed; at times she or he may need to handle group time or present a special activity. The diversity of the job responsibilities offers a stimulating and challenging work experience.

Directors function most effectively when they are comfortable delegating responsibilities to others. If you are the kind of person who feels you must do everything yourself, who is afraid to let others do some of the work, you will be an overwhelmed administrator, one who has too much to do. Capable administrators learn to share the burdens. In so doing, they not only relieve their own load but also communicate trust and community to the staff.

What are some of the personal qualities that the job of program director requires? A director of a large university program suggested that you need a real love and concern for children, but you also need to derive your major satisfactions from within yourself, as it is a very demanding profession. When you give to others all day long, it can be emotionally draining, and you don't always receive support from others. Those who find this job most rewarding are those who do have this built-in support system within themselves.

In all child-centered jobs you need good health and a high level of energy to meet the daily needs of both children and staff. A director of an early childhood program said you also must be able to tolerate a great deal of frustration. Again, you will need to rely on your internal reward system, as the job requires that you give a lot of support to others and may receive little back.

Let us look in detail at two unexceptional working days in the life of an early childhold center director.

8:00	Arrive at work.
8:05	Telephone rings. One of the teachers reports that she has the flu and cannot come to work.
8:07-8:15	Make calls to potential substitute teachers. The third one called agrees to come, but she can't get there until 9:30 (she's needed at 9:00).
8:15-9:00	Check children's health forms to make sure they are all in order. The licensing inspector will come in a week and will surely check them.
9:00-9:30	Cover for the ill teacher until the substitute teacher arrives.
9:30-10:30	Work on USDA food budget forms. (The center gets federal money to support meals. The money is welcome, but there is a lot of paperwork to be done.)
10:30-10:35	The telephone rings. The caller would like to enroll his child in the center. Explain that there are no openings, but you can put the child on a waiting list. Get the name and telephone number.
10:35-10:45	Another parent calls wanting to enroll a child. Explain that there are no openings. Parent starts to beg, plead, cry. Calmly, firmly repeat that there are no openings. Give her the telephone number of a center that might have openings.

10:45-12:00   The cook feels ill and asks if she can go home. Quickly prepare and serve lunch. Eat lunch with the children and then clean up dishes.

12:30-1:15   Interview a candidate for an assistant teacher job. Ascertain her philosophy of child care, her experience, and show her around the center.

1:15-1:30   Call the candidate's references. Ask for their candid opinions about her suitability for work in a day-care center.

1:30-2:45   Staff meeting while the children nap. Listen to and respond to problems. Help teachers find solutions. Discuss and plan the upcoming pot-luck dinner for parents and staff.

2:45-3:05   One teacher stays after the meeting to complain privately that she can't get along with her co-teacher. Discuss possible changes that could be made.

3:05-3:15   Call several plumbers to get estimates of the cost to fix three of the toilets.

3:15-4:30   Plan a workshop on music activities for young children. You have been asked to give the workshop at the next meeting of your local chapter of the Association for the Education of Young Children. Go home at 4:30.

The next day

8:30-11:30   Work on proposal to a state agency that may have funding for day-care centers. The funding would permit recruitment of a few low-income children and would allow for the replacement of some worn-out equipment.

11:30-12:15   A teacher brings in a sick child. You have him lie down on the couch in your office while you wait for his father to come get him. After comforting him, you continue to work on the proposal. You call your lunch partner to tell her you'll be late.

12:15-1:15   Go out for lunch with a friend.

1:15-2:30	Go to each teacher individually to ask her what new equipment she would like to have if the proposal you are writing is funded. Ask the teachers to give you information by tomorrow concerning the item's name, manufacturer, and cost.
2:30-3:30	Make a list of parents who owe money. Put "friendly reminders" in their children's cubbies.
3:30-4:15	Prepare payroll checks. (In bigger centers, secretaries handle this.)
4:15-5:30	A parent comes by the office. She is concerned because her child has started sucking his thumb and having nightmares since she and her husband separated. You discuss the child's feelings and help the parent think of some ways to help him through this difficult transition.

As you can see from these two hypothetical days, the director of a program for children is likely to be confronted with a lot of unexpected events. She does a lot of paperwork, a lot of helping others solve their interpersonal problems, and a lot of "filling in" during minor emergencies.

Advantages of a Career as Program Director

The major advantage of their job cited by many professional program directors is working with people. You will have the opportunity to work with children, parents, and teachers. You will also know that you are making a real contribution to children and their families through your child care program. Program directors find this exciting and challenging, as there are always new goals to accomplish. One director told us, "It is so important—what we do in the preschool years is so critical for children and families. It's exciting to be a part of." Another director described her satisfaction and rewards as she realized that for many young children her program provided the major stable support system in their lives, and she could see the positive changes occurring in the children through her program.

As a program director, you will continue to define your personal philosophy of children and families and will be in a position to evaluate their needs and concerns. You will therefore be able to communicate these needs and concerns to policy and decision makers. As you help to meet parents' needs by providing quality care and education for children, you will derive real satisfaction from your work. You *do* make a difference.

In this career you will be able to combine working with children and adults in an administrative capacity. Both skills will transfer to other career developments in the future. Additionally, jobs are usually available in any area of the United States if you have a bachelor's degree and some experience.

Disadvantages of a Career as Program Director

As in most child-centered occupations, salaries are lower than in other occupations requiring comparable training and experience. Although administrators receive higher pay than most early childhood centers, it is usually not a high-salaried career. One program director said that although she was paid about the same as an elementary school teacher, she was working eight hours a day instead of six and twelve months a year rather than nine.

Another director told us of the "strain and drain" of a high-pressure job that makes continuous demands of decision-making and support of others. The job has the potential for a high level of frustration each day. Since one of your primary responsibilities will be to give support to the staff, you may feel you have little left to give to others at the end of the day. One program director told us it was very difficult to face just one more interaction at the end of the work day. That may contribute to job turnover and burnout. As we interviewed two program directors of large day-care centers, they both said they felt that living alone contributed to their effectiveness on the job. They pointed out the difficulties those with families had, as they had so many more personal interactions at the end of the work day. All the directors we interviewed said it was important that you had support, and that this support was derived from two main areas: (1) from yourself, a built-in reliance on yourself and your capabilities; and (2) from your satisfaction in the importance of your work and your caring for children and their families.

Interviewing and Job-hunting Tips

Jobs for program directors are available all over the United States. In order to find the one that fits your career goals and qualifications, however, you may need to be willing to relocate. Good sources of job openings are your college placement service, newspaper listings, and a personal network of friends and professional colleagues. Many directors also establish their own centers after gaining experience.

It is important to accumulate experience in child care work, since an administrator must be familiar with all aspects of the center's operation.

It is also important for you to develop your own philosophy of children and families. You need to think this through carefully, as the board of directors who interview you will consider your philosophy as a major criterion in their selection.

You should be prepared to spend one-half to one day working with the children as a part of the interview process. In this way you can demonstrate your skills, capabilities, and flexibility, and it gives you an opportunity to observe the operation of the center and evaluate how it fits in with your goals and philosophy.

Professional organizations are an important part of a professional person's life. They enable you to interact and share information with your colleagues, and they provide continuing education. The major organization is the National Association for the Education of Young Children (NAEYC). In the southern United States, the Southern Association on Children Under Six (SACUS) is very active. Local chapters meet regularly and offer support and information on current developments in the profession.

In Chapter II we mentioned the possibility of finding good child care centers by looking into those that have met the requirements for national voluntary accreditation. You may want to do this as you apply for director positions. See Chapter VI for information on how to locate such centers. On the other hand, you may enjoy the challenge of improving a center that needs upgrading, or of starting your own center from scratch.

Chapter VIII

Child Life Specialist

Illness and disability and the medical procedures that are used often spell emotional as well as physical stress for children and their families. Sometimes the emotional problems that accompany medical care actually prolong or otherwise complicate the child's physical disorder. The mission of the child life profession is to meet the emotional and cognitive needs of children receiving medical care and to help their families make positive adjustments to the situation.

Most of the child life specialist's work occurs in pediatric health care settings (usually in hospitals). A typical day's activities for a child life worker might include comforting and distracting a hospitalized toddler who cries for his parents, setting up a doctor role-playing scene to help preschool and elementary school children understand what is happening to them, arranging tutoring for a child so that he doesn't fall behind in his school work, explaining to a teenager what the operation will be like and how she will feel afterwards, helping parents think of activities their child can enjoy while still in bed at home, and leading a discussion group for siblings of cancer patients.

The variety and the challenge of this profession are evident from these few examples. The job of doctors and nurses is primarily to reduce physical discomfort; often they do not have the time or the skill to help patients and their families with the emotional stress that may accompany illness, disability, and medical intervention. Meeting the emotional and developmental

74

needs of sick or disabled children and their families is the express job of child life specialists. They do so through the use of play, conversation, and other forms of communication. We will give more specific examples as we outline the roles that the child life specialist plays vis à vis children, the family, the rest of the health care staff, volunteers, and students.

First, the child. The child life specialist should know enough about the developmental needs of children of different ages so that she can anticipate their fears and emotional needs during illness and disability. She should be knowledgeable about techniques that can be used to reduce stress and enable children to see the positive aspects of their situation. Play is used a great deal. Props may be provided for the roles of doctor, nurse, child, parent, and so on, and children encouraged to act out the hospital scene. Board games such as Candyland or Monopoly can be modified to reflect the hospital layout. Puppet shows are often used as a way of comfortably describing hospital procedures to small children, as are appropriate storybooks and films. In some hospitals, video tape equipment is available so that adolescents can put together their own dramas. Hospitalized infants need someone who will simply cuddle and hold them. The tasks are many, and the child life specialist must be both skillful and flexible so that she can best meet the needs of the individual child, helping him to have as normal a life as possible while he is under medical care.

Second, the parents and siblings of the child patient receive advice and support from the child life specialist. Imagine the anxiety experienced by the parents and even by the brothers and sisters of a seriously ill or handicapped child. The child life specialist tries to support the family by listening to their concerns and explaining in layman's terms the medical procedures their child needs, by giving them practical ideas on how they can be involved in helping their child, and by directing them to other support services they may need. One of the most important things they do is to give reassurance. Thus, in at least one hospital, child life workers have made it their job to call parents of premature infants daily to report on their progress. In order to work with family members, child life workers arrange meetings in hospital and clinic waiting rooms, in homes, at the patient's bedside, in special afternoon or evening group sessions—in short, wherever and whenever their ingenuity takes them and families find convenient.

Child life specialists also interact with medical staff. In order to help patients and families, they must be aware of the diagnosis, the medical procedures to be undertaken, and the prognosis. Moreover, because they are likely to have a closer, more open relationship with the children than medical personnel do, they are in a position to sensitize the medical staff to the psychosocial needs of the child and family. For these reasons, child life specialists may go on rounds with doctors, attend staff conferences, and prepare charts or other written reports of their observations.

Child life specialists also work with volunteers and students. It is often the child life specialist who is called upon to train volunteers and students who want to work with children. These people are valuable resources for hospitals, but they need training to learn how to play with, talk to, and entertain children in ways that will benefit them. Child life specialists can provide that training and supervision.

Finally, in some areas child life specialists work with people in schools, outpatient clinics, and community groups to promote well children's understanding of health care and hospitals. The goal is to instill in children a positive attitude toward health care so that they will have a more positive experience when they do undergo medical treatment. Thus the child life specialist may be involved in helping teachers find suitable books and films, leading tours of the hospital for school children, and so on.

What are the pros and cons of being a child life specialist? Let us start with the positive aspects. First, as in other child care professions, one can find satisfaction from the knowledge that one is contributing to the welfare of children and families. Moreover, since child life specialists work with children and parents who are under stress, they have particularly great opportunities to help others. The child life specialists we talked to were excited about their careers because they felt needed, they enjoyed the children and parents, and they thrived on the constant challenge and variety of their work. Child life work does not suffer as much as some other child care careers from isolation and low prestige. Child life workers are in daily contact with other professionals, mostly medical personnel, social workers, and hospital administrators. That is quite different from the day-care worker whose only at-work contacts are with other day-care workers and parents. Although in many areas the hospital community has yet to accord the child life profession the esteem it deserves, it does tend to receive higher regard from the general community than most other child care professions. The salary, while not high, compares to that of an elementary school teacher. Day-care salaries, as we have already seen, are generally lower.

The child life specialists we interviewed were very enthusiastic about their jobs but, when asked, mentioned some drawbacks. One said that it is hard sometimes to cope with the realization that she can't possibly do everything she would like to do. "The needs of the children and families are so great. I feel so much responsibility, but I just can't do everything. Many times I go home drained. Then I play with my animals or take part in sports. My job is my whole life, but I have to have some other outlet so that I can relax and let out the frustrations."

Another problematic issue is that of prestige. Although the profession may enjoy higher social prestige than day-care professions, it suffers within the medical community. Not all hospitals even employ child life specialists, since many doctors and nurses are resistant to the idea that hospitalized or outpatient children need more emotional and educational support than they themselves have the time or inclination to give. Employment opportunities are best on the East and West coasts; more hospitals there are open to the idea than in the central United States.

The profession is young and still undergoing fundamental changes in credential requirements and what it is to be called. At present, the people who perform child life work are known in various hospitals as "recreation therapists," "activity therapists," or "play leaders." "Child life specialist" is the term preferred by the Association for the Care of Children's Health, but it is not yet universally recognized.

A number of colleges and universities have child life undergraduate and graduate programs. Undergraduate programs prepare one to work directly with children and parents; graduate programs prepare one for administrative and research duties as well as for direct contact with patients and their families. Among the courses offered are basic hospital procedures, the psychology of the ill or handicapped child, play therapy, art and music therapy, normal child development, and children under stress. Practicum placements are always required.

For up-to-date information about certification requirements and schools offering child life programs, write to:

The Association for the Care of Children's Health
3516 Wisconsin Avenue, NW
Washington, DC 20016

The Association also publishes a directory of American child life programs and a newsletter that contains an "Employment Opportunities" column. Its annual conference offers a job center where job openings are posted and applicants may display their résumés.

Chapter IX

Teaching Others About Child Care

The preceding chapters have focused on jobs that involve direct care of children. This chapter focuses on jobs that involve teaching other adults (parents, students, teachers) about child care. Some of these jobs bring one into regular direct contact with children; some (such as college instructor) do not. We will discuss careers in state extension and social work agencies, parent education programs, high school and college teaching and psychological therapy, and child advocacy.

Many people begin their careers working directly with children, then change to one of the jobs discussed here. One reason cited by people who have made this transition is that they got "burned out" after several years of working with children forty hours a week. They still cared about children but found themselves losing patience and enthusiasm, so they switched to a job that they expected to be less draining (although that didn't always turn out to be the case). Another reason people make the change is that the jobs described here tend to command higher salaries and greater prestige. Also by teaching adults, they feel they would be able to reach more children through them.

Parent Educators

Every person who works with children and families has the opportunity to be a parent educator. Teachers are parent educators when they influence parents to make changes in their attitudes and interaction styles. Social workers are parent educators when they help parents learn new ways to strengthen their families. Clergymen, psychologists, doctors, nurses, children's librarians, extension agents, all of these professionals serve as parent educators at one time or another. Here we shall outline parent education as a job in and of itself.

Parent educators are hired by private and public social welfare agencies, by school systems, by family day-care networks, by hospitals, and by private, state, federal, and university programs. In many areas parent educators whose background is similar to that of their clients are preferred. This means that college degrees are not necessarily required, and training occurs on the job. When parent education through home visits first became popular, this was not the case. However, it has been found that rapport is significantly better when the parents and parent educators share the same "language," which usually comes from having lived in the same community and having had many of the same life experiences. Previous formal education may be of little or no help. In fact, middle-class college-educated people have often done more harm than good because of the dogmatic belief that the kind of child-rearing they experienced or were taught was the only right way or because they could not hide their horror at poor living conditions.

What is a home visitor's work like? Most are responsible for making a number of visits to parents per week, coordinating with other services for the benefit of the families, and perhaps planning and leading group workshops or discussion sessions. Parents are encouraged and helped to improve their parenting and decision-making skills. Paperwork is always involved (reporting on one's activities; keeping regular records).

Working as a home-visiting parent educator can be tremendously rewarding, but it is not without its frustrations and difficulties. Successful home visitors love their work because they work with people who are needy, whose parenting skills may be very poor, and whose children can really benefit from the home visitor's influence. One of the nice things about the job is that some parents not only change but are grateful to you and express it. Thus, like all the careers described in this book, parent education appeals to people who want to make the world a little better. It is also an attractive option for people who want to do something for children but prefer to work directly with adults and indirectly with children, or with only one or a few children at a time. One benefit of the job that has been mentioned by a number of home visitors is that they themselves have gained in self-confidence and in interpersonal and coping skills. Said one, "I'm a lot better with my own kids now. I've learned a lot myself."

What are the difficulties associated with the job? For one, considerable travel may be involved, especially if you serve a rural or mountain area where homes are far apart. More serious is the fact that, particularly during the initial visits to a home, you don't know if you will be welcome or even if danger awaits you. For example, one home visitor told us of arriving at a home expecting to demonstrate to a young mother some ways of playing with blocks. Instead, the mother had forgotten the appointment and was out shopping. The husband invited her in to wait, and the home visitor accepted before realizing that the husband was drunk. As it turned out, she was not harmed, but there were some tense moments before she could get away.

Another frustration involves the fact that people and circumstances change slowly. One may feel overwhelmed by the problems facing a family and feel that change needs to be effected right away; yet it almost never is. A related concern of some home visitors is a feeling that they need more skills than they have. Usually, however, persons skilled in counseling techniques provide in-service training and are available to talk about specific problems. Finally, pay is typically fairly low.

To give you an idea of some typical activities of home visitors, let us list some that have been described to us:

- Visit homes weekly. Help parents understand normal child

development, give them concrete ideas for reading to their children, playing with them, arranging a predictable schedule for them.

- Arrange driving lessons for a mother so that she can become more independent.
- Enroll a child in a Head Start program so that he can gain in social skills and his mother can take high school courses.
- Drive a family to a medical appointment.
- Help organize a parent group.
- Take care of ten children for an hour and a half so the parent group can meet.
- Scavenge at lumberyards and stores for free "trash" that can be used in children's projects.
- Provide emergency first aid to children and parents.
- File child-abuse reports with social welfare agencies.
- Call the police to apprehend a father who has "kidnapped" his child.
- Attend training and support sessions with other home visitors.
- Attend to piles of paperwork.

As this list illustrates, while the primary goal of home visiting is parent education, in fact the home visitor must provide many other services as well. One cannot focus on the child and ignore the family's social context and the other issues they face. Children's lives will improve only as their parents' lives improve.

Another kind of parent educator is the person who subscribes to and presents packaged parent education programs such as Parent Effectiveness Training (PET) or Systematic Training for Effective Parenting (STEP). These programs furnish a curriculum that can be followed in leading a group of parents in workshops on family relations, communication, interpersonal relations, and discipline. In PET, for example, parents learn how to communicate with their children without blaming or moralizing. Positive techniques such as active listening, reassuring, and cooperative problem-solving are learned.

College teaching means many things: teaching children, teaching college students, and conducting research.

To become a parent leader using one of these programs, one must write for program materials such as books, manuals, cassettes, charts, cards, and brochures, and (for some programs) participate in training under an already trained leader. There is some cost for materials, usually around $100. The parent educator who uses one of these packages outside of an already existing program may also have to advertise in order to recruit parents. Parents are charged a fee, and this fee (minus expenses) is the income of the "free-lance" parent educator.

This mode of parent education shares some of the same pluses and minuses of home visiting with the following differences: In general, the parents have made the decision themselves to attend (and pay), so they are likely to be motivated to make changes. Also, you and a *group* of parents meet together, so parents can support each other and give each other advice; the leader doesn't have to do all the work. There are disadvantages as well, however. For one, there is no assurance of a steady income. The parent educator who uses one of the packages outside of an agency program is therefore likely to do it on the side, in addition to some other form of employment. Another frustration for some people is that the leader may not have a chance actually to see what goes on in his clients' homes; also he treats only one part of the system—the parents. For people who prefer a more intimate relationship with children and parents, home visiting may therefore be better. Another issue mentioned by some parent educators is the fact that many of the programs are only suitable for highly verbal middle-class families. Persons wanting to work with other clientele may therefore be frustrated.

The personal qualities, skills, and expectations that are appropriate for parent educators include the following:

- Sincere interest in children, in parents, and in helping parents improve their child-rearing skills.
- Knowledge of positive child-rearing skills and the ability to demonstrate them.
- Acknowledgment that parents, not the parent educator, are children's most important teachers.
- Acceptance of different cultures and ways of doing things.
- Good communication skills, including individual counseling and group facilitation skills.
- Knowledge of community agencies and other organizations that may be able to help clients.
- Ability to help parents feel more in control; this means taking pains not to make decisions for parents, but instead giving them enough support and information so that they may make their own.
- Sensitivity.
- Friendliness.
- Emotional maturity, strength, stability.
- Patience.

As you read on, you will see that most of these attributes are common to all of the careers described in this chapter.

Teacher of Child Development
at the High School or University Level

Another group of professionals who teach others about child care are junior high or high school teachers and college/university instructors or professors. Teaching at the high school level is quite different from teaching at the college level, so we will describe the two in turn.

To teach child development in a public junior high or high school, one generally needs teacher certification, earned by obtaining a bachelor's degree with credits from education and child and family development courses. Since teachers are likely to have to teach child development in conjunction with nutrition, home management, family living, and cooking and sewing, a degree in Home Economics Education is desirable. Financial considerations make it too expensive for most school systems to employ persons who can teach only child development. The teacher is generally identified as a home economics teacher. The child and family development courses taught are likely to include discussion of issues in family living, an overview of child development, and, increasingly, some actual hands-on experience with children for the students. This field experience may take place in neighborhood preschools, or a high school may have an on-site preschool where students receive practical training. The teacher must therefore be capable of doing demonstration teaching with young children, as well as supervising, observing, and talking to teenagers. Family living courses usually involve learning about and discussing intimate relationships and practical approaches to common family and friendship problems. Teachers should be able to approach tough issues matter-of-factly and with sensitivity.

Besides knowing their subject areas well, teachers should be sensitive persons who can communicate effectively with young people. One home economics teacher told us that she thinks one has to have a firm conviction that some of the information is getting through and will stick with students. "Adolescents," she smiled, "can seem so goofy. Sometimes my words seem like water off a duck's back. But some are really interested, and lately I've had former students come back and tell me my class made a lasting impact on how they are as parents. That makes it worth it." Teachers are also being heartened of late because an increasing number of boys are electing classes in child development and family living. "I'm so encouraged by this trend," said one teacher; "we used to have only girls. But how can you really have much impact on the family if you only speak to one of the sexes?"

Teachers also like the fact that they work only nine months of the year. However, dedicated teachers find that they have so much after-school work (grading, planning, attending faculty meetings, supervising student activities) that they end up working more than a 40-hour week while school is in session. "It looks like a job that lets you go at 3 o'clock every day, but it really isn't," advised one teacher. Furthermore, in some states teachers' pay is relatively low, so some teachers work at other jobs during the summers in order to meet their financial obligations.

Another problematic area for home economics teachers is that of prestige. The whole field of home economics, which really involves the generation and application of knowledge for the betterment of individual and family life, suffers from negative stereotyping. People who know little about it associate the field with learning to cook, sew, and baby-sit, subjects for "dumb girls." Much reeducation will have to occur before the general public understands the true meaning and mission of home economics. At any rate, home economics teachers inevitably feel this status problem, as do their students.

People who teach child development at the college or university level usually work in departments of child and family development, education, psychology, or nursing. Junior (two-year) college instructors typically need a master's degree; college faculty have either a master's (instructors) or a doctorate (assistant professors and above). As a rule, junior college instructors have fairly heavy teaching loads; college and university faculty may have lighter teaching loads, but they are required to do research in addition to teaching, attending meetings, participating in committee work, supervising student activities, and advising students about courses and careers. It is more than a full-time job; it is a career with responsibilities that can keep one busy all one's waking hours. "My work is on my mind all the time," explained one assistant professor; "even when I'm in the shower, I'm thinking about tomorrow's lecture or the article I'm writing, or how to get funding for my research."

College faculty teach others about child-rearing in several ways. Most obviously, their lectures to classes contain information about chld-rearing methods. Second, many departments of child and family development operate on-site child care programs for the purpose of teacher training. Programs for children aged 3 and 4 are most common, but a growing number of colleges and universities are adding infant-toddler and after-school (ages 5 to 11) programs. Typically, an instructor works in the program, caring for the children and teaching the student teachers. It is a demanding job. Let us look at one day in your life if you were an instructor in a university child development program, working in the preschool day-care room.

7:30 a.m. Arrive at work. With a student, take chairs down and quickly tidy the room.

7:45 a.m. The first children arrive. Greet the parents and children. Help the student help the children get involved in quiet activities.

8:00 a.m. Another student arrives, as do more children. Send one student to the kitchen to get breakfast. (A cook prepares it, but someone has to go get it.) Talk to a group of children about the activities planned for the day. Keep an eye on the student teacher so feedback can be given later.

8:30 a.m.   Breakfast. Each student heads a table; you observe from the observation booth, taking notes on the students' ability to facilitate conversation and good manners. Later talk to them, telling them what was good and what needs improvement.

9:00 a.m.   Lead half of circle time, then have a student lead the other half.

9:15 a.m.   A third student arrives. Each student takes a group of six children for planned table activities. You observe and give suggestions or intervene when necessary.

9:45 a.m.   The paid teaching assistant arrives. Free play begins. You do some model teaching.

11:00   You demonstrate how to help children clean up their toys. The student who came at 7:45 leaves.

11:15   The assistant teacher takes over, supervising story time and getting tables ready for lunch. You go to your office for private conferences with two students.

11:45   You join the class for lunch.

12:00   Two students leave; two others come in. You greet and orient them.

12:15   Help get cots ready for naptime. Help children brush their teeth and settle down to sleep.

12:45   Spend fifteen minutes getting together last-minute items needed for your lecture-workshop.

1:00   Hold a one-hour class with beginning practicum students.

2:00   Spend an hour making charts, planning field trips, writing lesson plans, ordering toys, or whatever else is necessary.

3:00   Help awaken children, make sure they use the toilet, get snack ready.

3:30   Leave for home. Your assistant teacher stays to supervise until 5:30, when the center closes.

Evening   Grade papers, prepare lectures or workshops, attend local meetings, etc. etc.

As this schedule indicates, the responsibilities of the instructor charged with practicum teaching are varied and include a great deal of interpersonal exchange with children, college-aged students, and parents. Not so evident is the fact that the instructor may also have much of the responsibility for keeping the child care room neat, the snacks nutritious, the parent program positive. In other words, a lot of practical details not usually associated with college teaching must be attended to. The fact that one not only runs a child care program, but also directs student teachers, makes the job more demanding than working as a teacher in a day-care center. One must address and cultivate two different audiences. Often it is not easy to attend to both at once. "When I first started teaching here," remarked one instructor, "I could focus on only one or the other. I would get so busy working with the children, I'd forget about the students. Then I'd feel guilty because I wasn't giving them any feedback. No wonder! I wasn't even seeing them! I'm better at it now, but it's still a juggling act."

Nonetheless, the job is a coveted one and has many positive aspects. We list some here:

- College- or university-based programs usually have more money for salaries and equipment than the average child care center.
- Accessibility to therapists, special entertainers, and other human resources is likely to be easier.
- The program for children is often richer because there are so many people (students) responsible for planning activities. Also, the enthusiasm of students, who haven't encountered burnout yet, can be uplifting.
- Being in a university community enables one to meet interesting people, both in and out of the field.
- One can sustain a feeling of really doing something to improve students' child-rearing skills. The course may have a lasting impact.

- Unlike many faculty members, one gets to see real life daily and to know children intimately.
- The pay and prestige levels, while not high, compare very favorably with those of other kinds of child care work.
- Compared to teaching in high school, problems of discipline and student motivation are lessened.

Other, less intensely involving, ways in which university faculty teach others about child care include supervising students in practicum placements in child care centers in the field (this involves giving regular workshops plus observing students' work in centers near the college), including child care information in lectures, sharing information with others at conferences and meetings and through books and articles, and serving on child care center boards. Faculty who do research also contribute to knowledge about the development of children and about effective child care methods.

Personal characteristics and abilities that are important for high school- and college-level faculty include:

- The ability to relate well to adolescents, young adults, and peers.
- Thorough knowledge of one's subject matter. For university faculty especially, this means knowledge of child and family development theory and research, research methods, and statistics.
- Excellent oral and written communication skills.
- Willingness to put in long hours.
- A genuine commitment to one's field, a personal identification with it.
- Assertiveness.
- Creativity.
- The ability to set realistic personal priorities and live by them. (Supervision is usually not close.)
- Perseverance, persistence. Teaching and research take much patience. Students often need a lot of attention

before they understand a point, and research involves a tremendous amount of detail. One must be willing to see small items through to completion in order that larger issues can be addressed.

We have discussed the specific advantages and disadvantages of work in a university child care program. Other faculty positions that do not involve as much (if any) hands-on experience with children have some of the same advantages and disadvantages. The level of pay and the level of status associated with university teaching are generally fairly adequate. The work is interesting and challenging, and one can enjoy a great deal of independence in thought and work habits. Being in a field like child development or psychology or education, one may also have the satisfaction of feeling that one's work is both theoretically and practically relevant. The fact that many appointments are for only nine months of the year is also appealing. Many faculty members do not take a three-month "vacation" but find it satisfying to have the time to attend to research and writing with minimal or no obligation to students.

On the negative side, for many, the job requires too much work and stress, particularly during the first years. The tenure system makes the first five years a "trial run" for assistant professors. During the sixth year, he or she is judged to be either worthy or not worthy of tenure. Judgments are made on the basis of the assistant professor's record in teaching, research, and service to the college or university. Those who are granted tenure have permanent job security. Only under extraordinary circumstances (such as budget crises) may persons with tenure be dismissed. If tenure is denied, the person may continue in the position for only one more year. Knowing that one's professional life may depend on those sixth-year evaluations can make the first five years particularly difficult.

The road to jobs in higher education is through graduate school. Most graduate programs emphasize the understanding of theory and research, the generation of independent research efforts, and the application of knowledge. Job openings for faculty must, by law, be announced nationwide. Good sources of information about open positions include university department bulletin boards and notebooks (notices are often sent to the appropriate departments in universities across the nation), university placement offices, and publications such as the *Chronicle of Higher Education* (1333 New Hampshire Avenue, NW, Washington, DC 20036). National or regional conferences usually have rooms set aside for posting job announcements, exchanging résumés, and interviewing. Interviewing on campus (essential for most positions) is likely to be fairly strenuous. The candidate is expected to present a seminar to faculty and students and to speak individually or in small groups to all faculty members in the department and the deans of the college. Competition for positions is keen, particularly as declining student enrollment has forced colleges and universities to cut back on faculty positions and as the number of qualified applicants for these positions has increased. Despite its stresses, the virtues of the university faculty position clearly place it in high demand.

Extension Work

Every American state and territory and the District of Columbia has a cooperative extension program. The mission of extension is to take the information produced by scientists at universities and research centers, translate it into practical and understandable terms, and transmit it to the public. The purpose of this educational effort, as stated in the 1983 Cooperative Extension Service report, is "better agriculture, better homes, better communities—in the aggregate, a better world."[1]

The national headquarters of the Cooperative Extension Service is in the U.S. Department of Agriculture in Washington, DC. The 3,000 local offices are based in state land-grant universities and county governments.

---

[1] *"Extension in the 80's": A Perspective for the Future of the Cooperative Extension Service.* A report of a joint committee of the U.S. Department of Agriculture and the National Association of State Universities and Land-Grant Colleges.

A state extension specialist demonstrates muscle tensing at a workshop on stress management.

Extension hires professionals and paraprofessionals to do its work. In this section we outline the responsibilities of extension home economists, child and family development specialists, and 4-H youth specialists. For the sake of perspective, however, you should keep in mind that extension also involves the work of specialists in agriculture, family economics and management, textiles and clothing, nutrition, housing and interior design, business, and industry. In many instances, child and family development specialists work with specialists in other fields to develop programs and answer questions.

Extension is organized differently in different states, but the basic employment structure includes state and area specialists. Each state (and territory) is divided into regional areas, each of which has an extension office. Area specialists are the people who work out of these local offices. Many local offices are able to hire specialists who serve that particular region or area only; however, budgetary constraints in some locations have made it necessary for each specialist to cover two or more areas. There are also state-to-state and even area-to-area differences in the degree of specialization asked of employees. In some areas, for example, there is one agent who is a child development specialist, another who is a nutrition specialist, and so on. In other areas the demand is for home economists whose training is broader, spanning at least two of the fields of home economics (family economics and home management, textiles and clothing, nutrition, housing and interior design, and child and family development). The area specialist position usually requires a master's degree; however, if you have held a closely related job before and if you are willing to live in a "less desirable" rural area, you may be able to get a job with only a bachelor's degree. In some states, people with bachelor's degrees are hired as assistants. An assistant in child development or youth work might be involved in doing background organizational work such as finding meeting places, in presenting packaged programs, and in making home visits to families.

The *area* child and family development specialist (master's degree) works directly with families and with people who work with families. It is his or her job to determine and respond to the needs of the local population in order to "improve the quality of life for individuals and families through enhancement of their economic and social well-being." Extension agents seek to do this through education. One area specialist with a master's in child and family development recalled a number of activities she had participated in during the last few months:

- Gave a talk on parent-teenager communication to a church group.
- Gave a talk on toddler negativism to a neighborhood group of mothers who had requested that she come to their monthly get-together.
- Wrote a regular newspaper column on child-rearing issues.
- Gave several radio and television talks on good Christmas presents for children.

- Issued a press release on new regulations regarding the reporting of child abuse.
- Worked with a nutrition specialist to develop a program on nutrition during pregnancy that would be understandable to the semiliterate.
- Together with a clothing specialist, coordinated a program on clothing for handicapped toddlers to be presented to a group of visiting nurses.
- Joined with the local public health service to provide support and child-rearing advice to parents waiting in clinic waiting rooms.
- Responded to innumerable telephone calls from private persons asking questions about child-rearing and family life, from what to do about diaper rash to whom to call about a teenager's suicide attempt.

This short list illustrates the diversity of the area child development specialist's activities. Note that the area home economist shoulders an even broader spectrum of duties, since he or she might be called upon to do all the activities listed plus answer questions about the proper temperature for pickling and what curtain fabric to buy for maximum insulation.

Another component of area extension is 4-H, the well-known youth education program. It is not directly concerned with child care, but we mention it here because it employs people with educational backgrounds in child and family development. 4-H staff develop programs and train volunteers to work with children aged 6 to 18. Although 4-H began by focusing on rural youth and still has a strong agricultural component, in recent years it has also begun to address the needs of urban youth and nonagricultural issues. For example, a 4-H agent might help coordinate and train local volunteers to hold workshops for teenagers on baby-sitting or on peer counseling skills. The programs are meant to supplement, not substitute for, regular school offerings.

State extension specialists are generally based in the extension offices of state land-grant universities. In most cases, state specialists have less direct contact with the public than do area specialists; their job is to help and support the area specialists with program development. They are expected to understand basic research in their field, to know how to put research findings into language that the public can understand, and to see and communicate the practical implications of research. The area specialists depend on the state specialists for this information. State specialists thus must read to keep up with new developments in their field, plan and hold training workshops for area specialists, and write newsletters condensing recent research findings. They spend a lot of time talking on the telephone and in person to the area specialists. Considerable travel is involved. They are also likely to appear on radio and television and to write newspaper columns and press releases. Coordination with other agencies is another responsibility. One state specialist we talked to, for example, was coordinating workshops for single parents with the state mental health agency. Another spoke of coordinating efforts with Head Start to develop in-service training for teachers. Sometimes the work of state extension specialists does take them directly to the public, but that is most likely to occur when they want to model a new approach to local staff. One state specialist told us that she particularly enjoyed these opportunities because they permitted her to get a real feel for the needs of the local population and, therefore, for the needs of the area specialists.

As a rule, the position of state specialist requires a PhD. In some states, such as New Hampshire, generalists are preferred, people with broad home economics backgrounds. In other states, such as Missouri, specialists, for example in child and family development, are the ones usually hired.

What are the advantages and disadvantages of extension work? All of the extension agents whom we interviewed expressed tremendous personal satisfaction with the opportunities they had to make a significant impact on families. "I know

I've helped a lot of parents change. Yesterday I showed a group of new mothers how to bathe an infant. I know I made a difference. I truly believe that parents can be reeducated," enthused one area specialist. "I feel like a missionary," said another. "I love to see positive change; I know I'm really helping." Other positive aspects of extension mentioned included dealing with real human issues, not just theoretical ones, the flexibility of the job, the challenge of taking information from the university and getting it into a form that people can understand and use, and the opportunities to work with other professionals, the real leaders of local communities. "You get to work where the paddle hits the water. This work is real, not a play job. I'm helping people make the most of it," summed up one state child development specialist. Also a plus is that the job usually pays relatively well.

What are some typical frustrations of extension jobs? To some extent, they are similar to those of all of the helping professions: not enough time, not enough money, not enough resources to meet all of the needs one sees. Like organizations in any field, some agencies are marked by poor organization, and staff do not have a good idea of what they are supposed to do and why. This can be a particular problem when the staff members have low initiative and cannot come up with ideas themselves. Extension specialists also noted that meeting real life head on isn't always easy or nice. "I still haven't quite gotten used to being yelled at by an irate parent or having to sit on a urine-soaked couch in a poor home." Another child development specialist who had worked in a home-based parent training project admitted, "It's hard talking to parents who have abused their children when you don't believe in spanking at all. I'm always a little afraid of what will happen if the parents aren't interested in what I have to say. Or if the group disagrees with me. Will I be able to defend my position? I used to get depressed because I wanted people to change overnight. Now I'm more realistic. I know it takes time. Sometimes I still get really upset by the living conditions of some of my clients. I didn't know before that some people in America don't even have floors. But I also get a big lift from helping people, so the job has a lot more 'ups' than 'downs'."

Another aspect of extension work that poses a problem for some is the amount of travel and the number of evening and weekend meetings involved. Area specialists move about extensively throughout their areas, and state specialists throughout their state. Particularly for people with small children, nights spent away from home can be a real difficulty. "I was lucky," remarked one specialist. "I didn't get into extension until my children were teenagers, and my husband was really good with them. They were fine without me. Younger families have a harder time."

What personal characteristics and abilities does one need for extension work? Here are some:

- A firm grounding in one's subject matter and knowledge of where to go to find out what one doesn't know.
- A commitment to keep up with the latest developments in the field.
- Good oral and written communication skills.
- High commitment to helping people make basic changes in their lives; a deep-down belief that one is making, and should make, the world a little better for others.
- Willingness to work more than a forty-hour week.
- Willingness to travel.
- Organization with flexibility. One must be organized, but at the same time able to make changes to meet perceived changes in people's needs and priorities.
- The ability to read one's audience, to adjust one's delivery depending on the listeners.
- Initiative, the ability to make independent decisions.
- The ability to work together with other professionals toward a common goal.
- Sincere respect for other people despite differing values and life-styles. People will sense it and be turned off if you

look down at their way of life. You must be capable of accepting and liking people as they are, from the "classiest to the most illiterate," as one specialist put it.

• General friendliness.

• The ability to make basic knowledge palatable to people who fundamentally disagree. For example, one will lose an audience that has believed in "spare the rod and spoil the child" for generations if one unequivocally condemns spanking. Sometimes one must be able to compromise one's values a little in order to guide people toward change.

• Patience. It takes time to effect real changes.

• Assertiveness.

What kinds of training prepare one for extension work? Clearly, a solid education in one or more subject areas is essential. Most specialists today hold master's or doctorate degrees. Also helpful, although not required, are courses in journalism, public speaking, and group facilitation skills. Some of those skills can be learned on-the-job and through in-service training, but employees who start work already having them have a head start.

If you are interested in working for extension and want to know more about the service in your area, contact your County Extension Center. You will find it listed in the telephone directory under county government listings. University placement offices post job announcements; one may also be able to find openings by following newspaper want ads. Extension offers many opportunities for volunteers, particularly within 4-H. You may find it worthwhile to do some volunteer work to get a taste of the work and to meet people who may be good contacts later.

Social Work

The term "social work" describes a variety of jobs and an equal variety of responsibilities. All of them, however, have one primary goal: to help people with social, emotional, or financial

A social worker and a Head Start teacher meet to plan coordination of services.

problems to help themselves. Social workers do this by working directly with persons and groups and by establishing and organizing community resources for people in need. Employment for social workers who teach parents and other professionals about child care can be found in a number of program areas: child abuse, family counseling, family services/foster care, mental health, probation and parole, juvenile corrections, child welfare, school social work, child guidance, recreation, youth services, public health, birth control/abortion counseling, and alcohol and drug rehabilitation.

The particular assignments of social workers depend on the agency, the location, the major industries in the area, the type of population being served, and the social worker's experience, education, and rank. Some social workers concentrate on direct service to people, other have more administrative, supervisory duties. Some typical activities that might fall to a caseworker who works directly with families include:

- Helping a newly disabled father apply for food stamps; arranging for counseling to help him learn to cope with his anger and guilt at not being able to provide for his family anymore.
- Counseling a mother about birth control, referring her to a public health agency for treatment.
- Giving information about a runaway child to the police.
- Helping parents find and use services for a handicapped child.
- Responding to reports of child abuse: helping to determine if abuse occurred, removing the child if he is in danger, arranging for counseling for the parents, doing some counseling oneself.
- Evaluating families who wish to become foster parents; placing children in foster care.
- Helping poor families get the services and money they are entitled to.
- Counseling parents about discipline problems or whatever other issues are important at the time.
- Coordinating services with other agencies.
- Writing reports on all that one has done.

Caseworkers generally work a forty-hour week, but many are on call during off hours, and some even wear pagers. Emergencies are common in social work.

A great many people are interested in finding social work jobs, but the rate of burnout is also high. Let us look at some of the pluses and minuses of the profession. The pluses are probably obvious, the principal one being the satisfaction that comes from helping others in need. Interaction with other professionals can also be stimulating. Not unexpectedly, the job also has its fair share of frustrations. Those shared with us include regulations and red tape that impede or slow down services needed immediately, inertia and lack of understanding on the part of clients, the sense that at times one is actually in physical danger when visiting homes, and the amount of paperwork that is required. For many, there is also emotional fatigue that comes from constantly being in the midst of other people's problems. It is especially difficult to witness others' distress knowing that one's ability to help is limited by insufficient time, money, and skill, bureaucratic regulations, society's prejudices, and so on.

Effective social workers suggest that the following abilities and personal qualities are necessary to do the job well:

- Maturity and stability; the ability to be immersed in other people's problems without becoming either too emotionally wrought up or too cold and unfeeling.
- Genuine liking and respect for people.
- Tolerance for people who live and think differently.
- Strong desire to help others.
- Ability to work as a team member.
- Objective good judgment.
- Flexibility.
- Patience.
- Sense of humor.
- Tact.
- Energy.
- Tolerance for ambiguity and confusion.
- Careful organization.
- Efficiency.
- Knowledge of other community resources (employment counselors, child placement agencies, lawyers, teachers, public health clinics).
- Counseling skills.

It is still possible to get a job as a social service aide or technician without a bachelor's degree. Life experience and knowledge of the community are all that is necessary for aides. Social service technicians also do not need a bachelor's in social work; they are hired after completion of an associate of arts degree or a bachelor's in another discipline. Social service aides and technicians relieve social workers of routine tasks such as filling out forms, answering the telephone, and so on.

Some years ago, a bachelor's degree in social work or social science was sufficient to get a job as a social worker. This is still true in some parts of the country, particularly in rural areas. Increasingly, however, a Master's Degree in Social Work (MSW) is required. Those who want to focus on children and child-rearing find that an undergraduate major in child development or psychology and some graduate courses in those areas are extremely helpful. A doctorate is usually required for teaching positions at the college level.

Specific information about bachelor's and graduate degrees in social work is available from:

Council on Social Work Education
1744 R Street, N.W.
Washington, D.C. 20009

Help in defining and finding jobs may also be obtained by writing to:

Social Work Careers Information Service
National Association of Social Workers
7981 Eastern Avenue
Silver Springs, MD 20910

Job listings are available in college placement offices, local newspaper want ads, and professional publications. Useful listings can be ordered by writing to the following: (There is a charge for most of these.)

Social Service Jobs
10 Angelica Drive
Framingham, MA 01701

APA Monitor
American Psychological Association
1200 17th Street, NW
Washington, DC 20036

NASW News
National Association of Social Workers
7981 Eastern Avenue
Silver Spring, MD 20910

Help Kids
Child Care Personnel Clearinghouse
P.O. Box 548
532 Settlers Landing Road
Hampton, VA 23669

New Human Services Newsletter
33 West 42nd Street
New York, NY 10036

Social Casework
Family Service Association of America
117 West Lake Park Drive
Milwaukee, WI 53224

Child Welfare
Child Welfare League of America
67 Irving Place
New York, NY 10003

As is the case with most of the child careers discussed in this book, work as a volunteer is an excellent way to obtain an inside look at social work. Many social agencies welcome volunteers; some provide them with training and give them considerable responsibility. For example, we know of college students who have worked as volunteers during summer vacations and have been trained to make evaluations of foster homes, to answer suicide hot lines, and to provide information, support, and comfort to clients in the waiting rooms of public health clinics. Such experiences provide excellent background for career decisions and also enable the young person to make significant personal contacts that could be useful later.

Counselors, Psychologists, Psychiatrists

Counselors, psychologists, and psychiatrists who work with parents, children, and teachers are also involved in teaching about child care. They do so in a variety of settings and in a variety of ways. School psychologists, for example, help students with social, emotional, and learning problems. To do so effectively, they must listen to, teach, advise, support, and enlist the help of parents and teachers. Counselors and psychologists in private practice or in social welfare or mental health agencies may be involved in helping parents understand the reasons for a child's misbehavior. Increasingly, industry is hiring counselors to help employees deal with family and other crises. Psychiatrists working through hospitals or their own private offices are likely to encounter similar needs.

What are the differences between counselors, psychologists, and psychiatrists? The differences are in educational background and in job responsibilities and privileges. Counselors usually have master's degrees in social work, psychology, or counseling. They work in schools, public agencies, and private offices. Counselors may handle early screening (by administering tests or through interviews) and psychological therapy through conversation, role playing, biofeedback, hypnosis, or any other means the counselor believes will be useful. In many ways, therefore, the counselor's work is similar to that of psychologists and psychiatrists, but his stature and income are usually lower. Most states do not require counselors to have any kind of license or to have had any specific training. Counselors therefore are quite diverse in their backgrounds.

The work of counselors and psychologists may be very similar, but the difference in job titles is nevertheless important. Psychologists usually have had more years of education and have received their degrees specifically from departments of psychology. Over 60 percent of American psychologists have doctorates. Not surprisingly, therefore, it is becoming increasingly difficult to get a job as a psychologist with a bachelor's or even a master's degree.

A license or certification is necessary in all states for psychologists who wish to go into private practice. Requirements differ from state to state; in general, however, to be licensed one needs a PhD, one or two years in an internship supervised by a licensed psychologist in one's area (e.g., marriage and family therapy, or child psychology), and a passing grade on an examination given by the state board of psychologists. Besides permitting one to practice privately, licensing is desirable from a practical standpoint because insurance companies generally will not make payments for therapy delivered by a nonlicensed practitioner. To find out specific details concerning licensing in your state, write to your state Board of Psychologists, a state mental health agency, the American Psychological Association (1717 K Street NW, Washington, DC 20006), or the American Association for Marriage and Family Therapy (924 West 9th Street, Upland, CA 91786).

After five years of experience, psychologists may apply for a diploma awarded by the American Board of Professional Psychology. To obtain this diploma, one must have a doctorate in psychology, professional endorsements, and a passing grade on an examination. Psychologists who wish to focus on children usually specialize in counseling psychology, clinical psychology, or school psychology. Counseling psychologists usually work with basically healthy, normal persons or families who are having trouble coping with family, work, school, or other problems. They work with people on a one-to-one basis, with whole families, or with groups. After using tests and interviews to arrive at an assessment of the problems troubling clients, counseling psychologists try to help them to change things in their own behavior or in the environment, or to learn to cope with things the way they are. Sometimes client and psychologist can arrive at a solution that involves a compromise between changing and coping. A key element is helping people understand why they think and act as they do. This usually involves a great deal of discussion about the client's childhood.

Clinical psychologists use many of the same basic approaches as counseling psychologists, but their clients are generally more seriously disturbed or depressed. Hospitals and mental health centers employ clinical psychologists to make personality assessments and to do therapy. Private practice is another option.

Both clinical and counseling psychologists are called upon to give advice to parents and others about child care. Parents often consult psychologists for help with discipline problems at home. Psychologists should know how to evaluate parent-child interactions and suggest changes to improve the relationship. In this way, the effective psychologist can have tremendous impact on the family child-rearing system.

School psychologists, who have master's degrees or doctorates in educational psychology, usually work in schools giving tests, helping teachers cope with behavior problems, and helping students with learning problems. As part of their work, they meet with parents and teachers in order to better understand their children's problems and to offer suggestions regarding treatment. Hence, they too are teaching about child care.

Psychiatrists must complete medical school, with specialization in psychiatry during the residency years. Unlike counselors and psychologists, they have the right to prescribe drugs (usually tranquilizers, antidepressants). Every psychiatrist is affiliated with a hospital that has psychiatric facilities. Ironically, psychiatrists may have less training in psychology and counseling techniques than counselors and psychologists. If teaching parents and other adults about child care is your career goal, psychiatry may therefore be a less successful choice than the other two. For more information on psychiatry, you may write for free booklets from:

American Psychiatric Association
1400 K Street, NW
Washington, DC 20005
(Ask for *"Careers in Psychiatry"*)

and

National Mental Health Association
1021 Prince Street
Arlington, VA 22314
(Ask for *"Focus"*)

Being an effective, successful counselor, psychologist, or psychiatrist takes a certain combination of personal qualities. Here are some mentioned by psychologists themselves:

- maturity, stability;
- objectivity;
- genuine interest in people and in helping them;
- interest in doing a lot of reading and in keeping up with new developments in the field;
- personal strength, assertiveness;
- a good sense of humor;
- understanding that change takes time; perseverance;
- high intelligence (needed for graduate school and for the actual practice of therapy);
- ability to work both alone and with others;
- excellent speaking and writing skills;
- high tolerance for frustration.

We interviewed several counselors and psychologists to find out how they view their careers. Perceptions differed depending on whether they were in private practice and, if not, the nature of the employing agency. One psychologist, for example, has an office in her basement. One reason she values her work is that she can work as many or as few hours as she likes. "I just had a baby, so now I see only two clients a day. It's an ideal part-time job." Those working in public agencies and hospitals, on the other hand, spoke of heavy workloads, tight schedules, short deadlines to meet, and long hours spent writing reports.

Of course, the main work satisfaction of psychologists comes when they feel they have helped someone through a difficult period. "It's so draining, sometimes, to live with other people's problems, but it feels so good when you know you've helped," said one. Pay is usually good, especially for those with doctorates and with thriving private practices.

The principal difficulty of the field is that it involves one deeply in other people's problems, and that can be wearing, especially for very caring persons. Psychologists say that they develop thicker skins as they become more experienced, but that has its dangers, too. One doesn't want to become too unfeeling. Also frustrating for some is the fact that change may come very slowly—a theme that is recurrent in this book. It takes a patient person to "make it" in any of the careers we describe.

If you would like more information regarding careers in psychology, write to:

Order Department
American Psychological Association
1200 17th Street, NW
Washington, DC 20036

(ask for *Careers in Psychology*)

Public Inquiries (11 A-21), NCMHI
National Institute of Mental Health
5600 Fishers Lane
Rockville, MD 20857

(ask for *Careers in Mental Health*)

Chapter X

Child Care Prospects in the 1990s

Throughout this book we have surveyed the various ways in which parents arrange for the care of their children when they themselves need to be away from the home. Whatever the reason for the parents' absence—whether to work to support the household, to attend classes for further education, or merely to pursue personal interests—the cost of the care has always fallen on them. They had to pay the baby-sitter or meet the cost of the more formal child-care provider.

As these costs rose, meeting them became increasingly difficult even for families in the moderate income range. For poor parents, however, it was often impossible. They could not improve their economic condition by having the mother take a job because they could not afford any kind of care for their children while the mother was at work.

In the closing years of the 1980s the proportions of the problem increased enormously. According to the Bureau of Labor Statistics, in 1977 women in the workforce with children under the age of six numbered 5.5 million. By 1987 that number had risen to 9.0 million. The 1977 figure represented 40.9 percent of women in the workforce; the 1987 figure was an increase to 56.7 percent.

Concerning the children involved in the burgeoning problem, Bureau of Labor Statistics show that in 1977 children under the age of six whose mothers worked numbered 6.4 million, or 37.6 percent of all American children. By 1987 that number had reached 10.5 million, or 53.1 percent.

Many of these families, of course, had a working father as head of the household. In 1976 the median income of such two-earner families with children under the age of six was $15,809; by 1986 that income figure had risen to $34,017.

The growing phenomenon of the single-parent family, however, revealed a far different picture. In 1976 the median income of families headed by a working woman with children under the age of six was $5,414; in 1986 it was still only $9,913.

Under the current high cost of living, even the two-earner family has difficulty stretching its income to accommodate the expense of child care. The single working mother is already well below the poverty level and is unable to stretch her income. Her only alternative may be to trust to the assistance of a relative or a neighbor or to go or remain on welfare.

Many large corporations have observed the growing proportions of the child-care problem among their employees and have voluntarily instituted various kinds of programs to help them cope. It is estimated, however, that only 3,000 of the six million U.S. employers provide any assistance to workers who need child-care facilities.

The federal government itself is notable in its provision of child-care facilities for its women employees. The Department of Labor, for example, pioneered some twenty years ago with the first day-care center for its workers. The General Services Administration operates a well-equipped day-care center for its employees in Washington, D.C. Plans are under way to build such centers in federal buildings across the country, principally for the benefit of government employees.

Current Federal Involvement

At present the federal government expends almost $7 billion a year in forms of child care. Perhaps its most notable program is Head Start. Originally established to prepare disadvantaged children for elementary school, Head Start was later extended to children of middle-income families. These parents paid fees according to their income. The program was established under the Economic Opportunity Act of 1964. Studies of children who have been enrolled in it show a remarkable record of success in school.

Under legislation being considered by the Congress in late 1989, the Head Start program would be expanded to provide all-day care to preschool children all year round.

Another aid that the government offers to working parents is tax credits. Within certain limits, such parents can claim the costs of child care as deductions in the computation of their federal income tax returns. This advantage does not accrue to low-income parents, however, who are exempt from payment of income taxes. Among proposals for expansion of child-care benefits were several plans to make the tax credits refundable, thereby lending assistance to such low-income parents.

The federal government concedes that problems exist in the nation's child-care provision. Shortages of day-care centers are evident in some areas of the country, and the quality of the facilities that are available is not always of the highest. On the whole, however, government spokesmen hold that the difficulties are spotty in nature and not widespread.

The problem also encompasses the thorny controversy over government intrusion in the private sector. The administration firmly rejects suggestions that any kind of pressure be put upon business and industry to provide any form of child-care assistance to their employees.

As the largest employer in the United States, the government is willing to act as a model in the provision of benefits to its employees. In addition to the day-care center program previously noted, federal employees receive liberal parental benefits, including in some departments as much as a year of unpaid leave after the birth—or in some cases—adoption of a child.

The Department of Labor also is active in encouraging other groups in providing assistance to working parents. Technical advice is available to state and local governments, which are increasingly becoming involved in the child-care effort. Unions and community groups may also participate in the Department's information-sharing program.

State and Local Involvement

Many states are indeed taking up the federal challenge by establishing programs of assistance to working parents.

Local and county governments also are coming onto the scene with plans for their own employees and for workers in business and industry. Among such proposals, some in effect and some still under consideration, are the following:

- Requirement that all companies doing business with the county take steps to cope with the child-care needs of their employees.
- Authorization for parents to use accumulated paid sick leave to stay at home to care for sick children.
- Guarantee of unpaid leave—for either mother or father— to take care of a sick child or after the birth or adoption of a child.
- Requirement that developers of office buildings and hotels set aside adequate space for day-care centers or acquire such space nearby in the community.
- Establishment of day-care centers in elementary schools for toddlers and preschool children.

The Growing Debate

Both houses of Congress, business and industry groups, and concerned professionals align themselves on both sides of the question of federal assistance to working parents.

Supporters of federal involvement point to the fact that the serious problem of absenteeism in industry could be considerably reduced if working mothers had ready access to quality day care. Others maintain that the cost to the nation of not having available day care is greater than the cost of providing it. The unmanageable size of the welfare rolls, they hold, is largely the result of parents' inability to take jobs while they have small children at home.

These proponents point out that the United States is one of the few nations in the world that still have no program of assistance for low-income parents of small children.

Opponents of federal assistance warn that a national approach to child care would further damage the nuclear family in the United States. They argue that easy availability of child care would discourage mothers from staying at home and nurturing the family. They also point to the opinion of some psychologists and psychiatrists that programs of care outside the home are damaging to young children.

The argument also takes on political overtones. Legislators of both major parties can be found on either side of the question, with the disagreement running largely between conservatives and liberals among both Republicans and Democrats.

All factions tend to agree, however, that creation of a new federal bureaucracy is not the answer—in fact, is a course strictly to be avoided.

The most widely held recommendation is that of creating block grants to the states, which in turn would distribute the funds to public and private child-care centers or to developers of such facilities. Many observers favor establishments of tax credits for employers that provide day care for children of workers.

The administration continues to maintain that it can serve as a role model for business and industry in providing child-care facilities for its own employees, but it must not dictate to the private sector. It insists that any legislation that the Congress adopts must be directed only to low-income parents and must not adversely affect parents who prefer to stay at home and care for their own children.

The problem remains a thorny one with the capacity to arouse stormy controversy. No matter what the shape and scope of the legislation passed as the decade of the 1980s closes, child care is likely to challenge administrations and Congresses for years to come.

The Private Sector

Regardless of what action the federal government takes now or in the future, employers are increasingly coming to accept part of the responsibility for care of their employees' young children.

Many innovative plans are in operation or on the drawing board, including direct services, informational services, financial assistance, and flexible personnel policies.

Direct Services

Some companies establish on-site or near-site centers for child care. They may own and operate the facility, build the center and give it to an employee-operated group, or contract with an out-size organization to operate a center. Merck Pharmaceuticals, of Rahway, New Jersey, for instance, established and funded the Employee's Center for Young Children for three years, after which it was incorporated as a nonprofit center. It was later followed by a similar center at the Merck installation at West Point, Pennsylvania.

Consortium Centers

A group of employers, sometimes with a community agency, a union, or both, may establish a nonprofit corporation to fund a day-care center. An example is the Chinatown Day Care Center, in New York City. Initiated by the International Ladies' Garment Workers' Union, it is funded by the Greater Blouse, Skirt and Undergarment Association (an employer group) and a grant from the Job Training Partnership Act, administered by the Agency for Child Development of the Human Resources Administration. Children of employees are chosen by lottery. The parents pay weekly fees ranging from $2 to $55, depending on income.

In Philadelphia the Council for Labor and Industry established a private, nonprofit day-care center for employees of businesses within a ten-block radius of the center. Enrollment is now open. The center is subsidized by fees from the parents, by the state of Pennsylvania, and by voluntary contributions from employers such as Pennsylvania Bell and Strawbridge & Clothier.

Family Day-care Networks

Some employers contract with local agencies to recruit, train, and assist people to become licensed home care providers. This type of program may be especially appropriate for infants and may offer flexible hours for people who work odd shifts. For instance, the Family Planning Council of Norfolk, Virginia, is a private, nonprofit agency licensed by the Commonwealth to monitor private day-care homes. It contracts with area employers to refer employees. Parents may choose among homes in their area. The program is not subsidized, but employees of member companies may receive a reduced rate.

Emergency Services

One of the most difficult problems facing working mothers of young children is making emergency arrangements for care of a sick child at home. This problem has been attacked by a number of major employer firms. An example is Little, Brown & Company of Boston, a division of Time, Inc. The firm has contracted with a provider agency and in effect "buys a discount" for its employees by paying the difference between what the caregiver receives and what the provider agency charges.

In New York City seven major employers in 1989 joined together to provide home child care to employees whose regular arrangements go awry for any of various reasons.

The companies involved are Colgate-Palmolive Company; Consolidated Edison; Ernst & Young, an accounting firm; Home Box Office; National Westminster Bank, USA; the law firm Skadden, Arps, Slate, Meagher & Flom; and The Time Inc. Magazines Company.

Working with Child Care, a local resource and referral agency, the companies are participating in a one-year pilot program. Emergency care will be provided for well or mildly ill youngsters under the age of thirteen. The child-care workers will be provided by two licensed home health care agencies, Selfhelp Community Services of New York and Contemporary Home Care Services of Jersey City, New Jersey.

The employers' decision to provide home care rather than in a center was based on the commuting situation in the metropolitan area. Most employees travel a significant distance from home to work and would not want to have to travel with a child—especially a sick one.

The companies involved have yet to determine whether and how to subsidize the fees for employees. Questionnaires are to be given to employees after use of the service to assess its value.

Informational Services

Programs called child care resource and referral (CCR & R) are provided by employers or by contract with a community resource and referral agency. They inform employees about types of child care available in the community, which programs have vacancies, and specific facts about each service.

IBM established the first such network, which includes more than 150 community-based referral organizations. The service is free to employees; however, they make the final decision and pay for the care.

Financial Assistance

So far the greatest number of employers opt for helping employees pay for child care. This is done in various ways, including voucher or subsidy plans, discount programs, dependent care assistance plans (DCAP), and flexible or "cafeteria"-style benefits.

Among voucher plans, the Polaroid Corp. offers vouchers

worth 10 to 80 percent of child-care costs. The highest subsidy is paid to the lowest earners; the lowest subsidy to the highest earners. The Zayre Corp. in Boston reimburses up to $20 per week for child care expenses to employees of more than six months' tenure. The *Village Voice* newspaper offers $500 yearly for preschool child care. The plan is jointly funded by the paper and by District 65 of the United Auto Workers.

Some child-care centers, in conjunction with certain employers, offer a 10 percent discount on services, which is usually matched by the employer.

Flexible or "cafeteria" style benefits represent reorganization of companies' general fringe benefit plans to meet family needs. Employees may choose child care as one of a number of optional benefits, thus serving their purposes without increasing the total cost of benefits to the employer.

Under another option, employees may choose to exchange a portion of salary for a nontaxable child care benefit.

Flexible Personnel Policies

Some employers contribute to the child-care needs of employees by instituting flexible job policies, often without any increase in overall cost of benefits. These include flextime, sick child care leave, part-time schedules, job-sharing, extended maternity and paternity leaves, and work-at home plans.

The flextime option has been adopted by several companies in Philadelphia, including Community Legal Services. Employees set their own hours, provided they work a certain number of hours each day and during "core hours" determined by the employer.

Compressed time is an increasingly popular scheduling option among employees. The most common plan allows employees to work four ten-hour days a week, with three full days off.

Maternity and paternity leave is becoming widespread. American Telephone & Telegraph has a policy by which a mother receives up to eight weeks' paid leave. The mother and the father (if both work for AT&T) can take up to a year between them of unpaid but job-protected leave.

The Schools

A phenomenon of the increasing concentration on child care is the growth in the number of schools providing full-day kindergarten. At present the only two states that require the program are Florida and North Carolina, but many state school systems now offer it.

The programs have their champions and their opponents. Those who oppose hold that the purpose is merely to pressure the children to learn material that will be more suitable and better absorbed in first grade.

The proponents hold that if the programs do not stress "book learning" but emphasize direct experiences and handling of materials, the longer kindergarten day can be valuable to the five-year-old.

New York City has had full-day kindergarten since 1984, and it is considered highly successful. It is also highly popular with parents, who have developed confidence about the security and well-being of their youngsters. The once often-cited dangers of excessive fatigue for the children are being dissipated by the number of healthy, contented children who have undergone the program.

Chapter **XI**

Finding a Job

In each chapter of this book, we have made some suggestions that should help you decide what job you would like to pursue and how to go about getting it. In this chapter we deal very specifically with job-hunting and job-keeping strategies.

The first step, of course, is to decide what you want to do. Guidance counselors can help you with that decision. You might find it useful to take one of the vocational interest inventories that many placement centers offer. Some are like pencil-and-paper tests; others are easy-to-use computer programs. Most of them help you to become aware of your personal values, priorities, and interests and to match them with the jobs that seem to fit. High school and college placement offices usually offer this service free of charge.

But saying (or writing) that you "like children" and want to work with them is easy. We strongly suggest that you *try* working with children before you plunge into it as a career. Each of the professions described in this book welcomes volunteers. Even without prior experience or educational credentials, you will be more than welcome in most day-care centers, family day-care homes, hospital pediatric wards, summer camps, residential homes, and after-school day-care programs if you offer to work without charge for a few hours a week. There are several reasons why this is a good idea. First and most obviously, you will find out if you really do like working in this kind of setting, and you will learn some skills that will help you do so. Second, you will make some personal contacts that may prove very important in the future. Many times word about choice job openings trickles out by word of mouth before it ever appears in the newspaper want ads. Many of the people we interviewed, when asked how they found out about their job, said, "Oh, a friend told me about it." By working as a volunteer, you can start to get into this network.

Once you are fairly sure of the direction you want to go, find out how to prepare for it. Many people believe that some of us are born knowing how to work with children, that training isn't really necessary. We cannot emphasize enough how much we disagree with that position. Many of us can do a pretty good job entertaining one or two healthy children at a time, but working with sick or disabled children or with *groups* of lively children is a different story. The fields of child development and education have amassed much information on how to provide high-quality child care. As we have said before, you will have a better time and the children under your care will benefit more if you obtain and use a good child-centered education.

In most cases, there are several steps to job-hunting: writing a résumé, finding job openings in the area that you want, applying for the jobs, and being interviewed. We will offer some suggestions for each of these steps.

The Résumé and Cover Letter

The résumé is a summary of your educational and work history and interests. Your résumé is very important because it is usually the first and only thing a potential employer knows about you. The purpose of a résumé is to get you an interview: if the employer likes your résumé, he will want to see you. Even if you are the best thing that could possibly happen to children, you could miss out on some great jobs if you don't have a résumé that makes employers want to call you.

How do you do it? First, make sure that your résumé is straightforward, focused. Concentrate on communicating your goals and experiences that are relevant to working with children and families. Jobs that had little to do with child care can be omitted unless you need them to show that this will not be your first job. Make sure that your résumé is visually inviting; that means using an outline format, enough white space, even margins, perfect grammar and spelling, and usually limiting the document to one or two pages.

Some guidance counselors suggest that you have one résumé to fit each type of job you will apply for. Thus, you might have one that lists your goal as "day-care teacher" and another that makes you look like an aspiring child health specialist. This tactic is particularly useful if you have a heading called "Employment Goals" and couch those goals to suit each type of job you will try for. It's considered an acceptable practice for any person who is frankly searching for his or her niche; you don't have to feel you're cheating when you do it.

For details on how to write a good résumé, we suggest that you consult a career counselor or one of the numerous books and articles on the subject. Here we will give you some pointers that are specific to job-hunting in the child care area. We will also show you two résumés as examples of layout and wording. Our pointers:

- When you describe your education, list courses you have taken in child development, education, psychology, or related fields. If you majored in one of those fields, give the name of the major and where you studied. If you participated in any practicum placements, be sure to mention it.
- When you describe your past employment, be sure to indicate what you did, particularly as it related to management, child care, or communication with adults.
- If you ever did volunteer work with children or families, be sure to describe it. Several directors we talked to mentioned that they look upon volunteer work very favorably.

Two sample résumés follow. You may model yours after one

of them, but don't think you need to follow it exactly. These are just two of many possible formats. You may want to do some experimenting before you discover the layout that's perfect for you.

June Irwin

Current address and telephone:
>751 South 10th Street
>Columbia, Missouri 65201
>314-832-7961

Education
>University of Missouri–Columbia
>B.A., June, 1983
>Major in Child Development and Family Studies
>Practicum work: student taught in a university nursery
>>school (ages 2–5) and after-school pro-
>>gram (ages 5–10).

Employment
>Sunshine Day Care Center, St. Louis
>Assistant teacher, summer, 1982.
>
>The Gates Family
>>Provided baby-sitting for two small children, ten
>>hours a week, 1981–82

Jane Brown

Current address and telephone:
>345 West 85th Street
>New York, NY 10038
>212-571-3456

Employment goal:
Teacher of 3- or 4-year-olds in a day-care center.

Education,
New York University
Completed three years of undergraduate program, 1983.
Area of concentration: Psychology.
Relevant coursework: Psychology of early childhood.
Abnormal psychology
Child development laboratory

Employment
Frenchies Grill, New York City
Worked as a waitress, part-time, 1979–83.

Volunteer work
Tutored inner-city children in reading, 1979–81.
Worked at Hilltop Day Care Center ten hours per week,
1982–83.

References
Dr. Milton Samter, 325 Riverside Drive, N.Y., N.Y.
10025. Tel. 864-7676
Joyce Gregg, 18 W. 20th St., N.Y., N.Y. 10011. Tel.
777-9764

Notice that both résumés list essentials such as name, address, telephone number, education, and work and volunteer experience. Both are straightforward and easy to read. There are some differences, however. June is open to accepting one of a variety of child-care jobs. She isn't sure exactly what she wants. Jane is sure, and she indicates a specific employment goal. Or she prepares two or three résumés, each with a different goal. June completed a college major, which is self-explanatory. She doesn't have to list relevant courses, as Jane does, because the major, child development and family studies, is understood to include relevant practical and theoretical coursework. She does describe her practicum placement because she wants to be sure that potential employers know about it. Under the Employment heading, June lists only those jobs that relate to child care; she skips all the waitressing she has done. Jane, on the other hand, shows her waitressing job because she has had no other paid work. Another difference between the two résumés concerns references. Jane lists two specific people; June would rather hold off and give this information when asked. If you do give names and addresses of specific people, be sure to ask permission first.

Each time you send your résumé out, you should attach a cover letter. The cover letter should be written in standard business format and, if at all possible, addressed to a specific person, not a program or hospital. It is a good idea to call first to inquire to whom the résumé should be sent. In the cover letter, briefly summarize the major points of your résumé and indicate the position you desire. You may want to add some information, such as the name of the person who told you about the job opening (always a plus if the person reading the letter also knows and respects this person), why you would like to work for the particular program, and your special training or experience that qualifies you for this job. This is where you can sound enthusiastic and competent. End your cover letter with a request for an interview and a thank you. Be absolutely sure that your spelling and grammar are perfect. No matter what job you are applying for, poor writing skills will not look well. If you have trouble with writing, ask someone to review your letter before you type a final copy.

The Interview

For many people, the interview is the hardest part of job-hunting. Maybe it will comfort you to know that it is also hard for the interviewer, for she must think of the right questions and answers and try to put you at ease. You can make the process easier and increase your chances of getting the job by coming prepared. How do you prepare? First, by knowing something about the program, and second, by being able to articulate your philosophy of child care. Before you go for the interview, ask around about the program or center; find out as much as you can about the people and their approach. Then you will be able to ask intelligent questions and show a sincere interest in the program. The interviewer will think you know what you're getting into, always a good impression to make. Knowing something about the center, you will also be able to tune your answers and comments to the program and the position. This doesn't mean being dishonest; it just means remembering to say those things that you really feel and that the employer would probably like to hear.

Be sure to have thought about your philosophy of child care before you go. Programs differ widely in their approaches to children. Directors want to hear your philosophy to be sure it agrees with their own. Be thoughtful and honest as you speak. You will not be happy working in a program where you must contradict your own values, especially if you believe in them strongly. We know a graduate of a university department of child and family development who took a job in a day-care center where she was required to keep the room tidy at all times and to teach the ABC's. Her undergraduate program, on the other hand, had stressed the importance of active learning and spontaneous conversation. Her education had convinced her that the goals of this day-care center were inappropriate for preschoolers. "I finally quit. I just couldn't do it. I told the director I wanted to have fingerpainting and other such activities. She said it was too messy and that she wouldn't allow it. Now I'm job-hunting again." By the way, it is acceptable to take with you to the interview a "crib sheet" outlining your goals and philosophy. You can glance at it to help you remember important points as you talk.

Two other pointers. During the interview, don't say harsh things about the place where you are now working or where you worked before. One day-care teacher told us, "Yes, we interviewed her. I know you recommended her highly, but she was so critical of the day-care center where she worked before; we were afraid she'd be too critical of us, too. We hired someone else."

Second, don't say that you want the job because you "love children." (That could be one reason if you have many others as well, but it shouldn't be your one and only.) One employer commented to us, "When I hear, 'Oh, I love children!' or 'Children are so sweet!', I think this person is naive and inexperienced. Does she know what a whiney, tired child is like? I'd rather hire someone who sounds as if she really knows children, how they're wonderful, but also how they're not."

Leave discussion about salary, vacations, and other benefits to the end; some people even suggest putting this part of the negotiations off until the job is offered. That probably isn't necessary, but don't make it sound like your primary concern. Your primary concern is that you want to work with and for children.

The demand for people in child care is great. Recent figures show that almost 50 percent of mothers with children under six years of age work outside the home, and the percentage will continue to rise. Moreover, as one day-care director said, "There is always room for a person who is good with children." You can make that room for yourself in an established program, or you can establish your own (as family day-care providers do). Moreover, you can regard your position as the job you want to do always, or you can see it as a stepping-stone to other jobs. There is a great deal of job mobility among child care providers, both in child care positions and from child care positions to related careers that require more education—psychology, therapy, high school and university child development teaching. Child care is a fulfilling, worthwhile, and challenging area. Advocates are now working to improve its position in regard to money and prestige. We hope this book has given you a realistic view of child care options, the pros and cons.

Appendix

Child Care-Oriented Organizations and Agencies

Following are the names and addresses of the national (or international) offices of organizations concerned with child care and child care professions. Many of them have state or county offices; you may obtain local addresses by writing to the national headquarters.

American Academy of Pediatrics
P.O. Box 927
Elk Grove Village, IL 60009

Association for Supervision and
   Curriculum Development
125 N. West Street
Alexandria, VA 22314

Big Brothers/Big Sisters of America
230 N. 13th Street
Philadelphia, PA 19107

Family Service Association of America
117 West Lake Park Drive
Milwaukee, WI 53224

National Association for Child Care
   Management
1255 23rd Street, N.W. Suite 850
Washington, D.C. 20037

American Child Care Services, Inc.
532 Settlers Landing Road
Hampton, VA 23669

American Home Economics Association
2010 Massachusetts Avenue, NW
Washington, DC 20036

American Montessori Society
150 Fifth Avenue
New York, NY 10011

American Psychiatric Association
1400 K Street, NW
Washington, DC 20005

American Psychological Association
1200 17th Street, NW
Washington, DC 20036

Association for the Care of Children's
   Health
3615 Wisconsin Avenue, NW
Washington, DC 20016

Association for Childhood Education
   International
11141 Georgia Avenue
Wheaton, MD 29092

Association for Children and Adults
with Learning Disabilities
4156 Library Road
Pittsburgh, PA 15234

Association for Supervision and
Curriculum Development
225 North Washington Street
Alexandria, VA 22314

Big Brothers/Big Sisters of America
117 South 17th Street
Philadelphia, PA 19103

Boy Scouts of America
1325 Walnut Hill Lane
Irving, TX 75038

Catalyst Career and Family Center
250 Park Avenue South
New York, NY 10003

Center for Parent Education
55 Chapel Street
Newton, MA 02160

Child Care Action Campaign
90 Hudson Street
New York, NY 10013

Child Welfare League of America
67 Irving Place
New York, NY 10003

Children's Bureau
Administration for Children, Youth,
and Families
Office of Human Development
Services
U.S. Department of Health and
Human Services
P.O. Box 1182
Washington, DC 20013

Children's Defense Fund
122 C Street, NW
Washington, DC 20032

Council for Exceptional Children
1920 Association Drive
Reston, VA 22091-1589

Day Care Council of America
1602 17th Street, NW
Washington, DC 20036

Family Services Association of
America
44 East 23rd Street
New York, NY 10010

Girls Scouts of the USA
830 Third Avenue
New York, NY 10022

High/Scope Educational Research
Foundation
600 North River Street
Ypsilanti, MI 48197

National Association for Child Care
Management
1800 M Street, NW
Washington, DC 20036

National Association for the
Education
of Young Children
1834 Connecticut Avenue, NW
Washington, DC 20009

National Association of Social
Workers
7981 Eastern Avenue
Silver Spring, MD 20910

National Black Child Development
Institute
1463 Rhode Island Avenue, NW
Washington, DC 20005

National Camping Association
353 West 56th Street
New York, NY 10019

National Committee for Prevention
of
Child Abuse
332 South Michigan Avenue
Suite 1250
Chicago, IL 60604

National Congress of Parents and
Teachers
700 North Bush Street
Chicago, IL 60611

National Council of Churches
475 Riverside Drive
New York, NY 10115

National Council on Family
  Relations
1910 West County Road B
St. Paul, MN 55113

National Head Start Association
1707 15th Street, East
Bradenton, FL 33508

National Institute of Mental Health
5600 Fishers Lane
Rockville, MD 20857

National Jewish Welfare Board
15 East 26th Street
New York, NY 10010

Parent Cooperative Preschools
  International
P.O. Box 15604
Phoenix, AZ 85060

Society for Research in Child
  Development
University of Chicago
5801 Ellis Avenue
Chicago, IL 60637

Southern Association on Children
  Under Six
Box 5403
Brady Station
Little Rock, AR 72215

Student National Education Association
1201 16th Street, NW
Washington, DC 20036

Work and Family Information Center
The Conference Board
845 Third Avenue
New York, NY 10022

Work/Family Directions
200 The Riverway
Boston, MA 02215

Bibliography

Many books and articles have been written describing child care activities and programs. The books and journals listed below are ones that we have found helpful. Most of them cannot be found on the shelves of the average bookstore, but bookstore managers are generally glad to order a book for you. College and university libraries are likely to have copies of some of the books.

One of the best ways to get good but inexpensive books on child care is to order them through the National Association for the Education of Young Children. For a list of publications, write to: 1834 Connecticut Avenue, NW, Washington, DC 20009. We also recommend subscribing to its monthly journal, *Young Children*.

Two other good journals are *Day Care and Early Education* and *Child Care Quarterly*, both published by Human Sciences Press, Inc., 72 Fifth Avenue, New York, NY 10011. *Today's Child*, available through Today's Child Magazine, C N 5245, Princeton, NJ 08540, is an excellent monthly publication summarizing major research and political developments of concern to people in child care.

Information on a variety of topics, including curricula, is available from the ERIC clearinghouse on Elementary and Early Childhood Education, College of Education, University of Illinois, 805 West Pennsylvania Avenue, Urbana, IL 61801-4897.

Administering Day Care and Preschool Programs. D. Streets. Boston: Allyn & Bacon, 1982. $17.95.

An Activities Handbook for Teachers of Young Children. D.J. Croft and R.D. Hess. Boston: Houghton Mifflin Co., 1980.

Art for the Fun of It: A Guide for Teaching Young Children. Peggy D. Jenkins. Englewood Cliffs, N.J.: Prentice-Hall, 1980. $6.95.

Caring for Infants: What Works, What Doesn't. Vols. I and II. R. Neugebauer and R. Lurie, eds. Redmond, Wash.: Child Care Information Exchange, 1980, 1982. Vol. I, $7.70. Vol. II, $10.00.

Child Abuse: An Agenda for Action. G. Gerbner, C. Ross, and E. Zigler, eds. New York: Oxford University Press, 1980.

Child Life in Hospitals: Theory and Practice. R.H. Thompson and G. Stanford. Springfield, Ill.: Charles C. Thomas, 1981.

Developing and Administering Early Childhood Programs. V. Lombardo and E. Lombardo. Springfield, IL: C.C. Thomas, 1983. $23.50.

Diversity in the Classroom: A Multicultural Approach to the Education of Young Children. F.E. Kendall. New York: Teachers College Press, 1983. $8.95.

Early Childhood Programs and the Public Schools. Anne Mitchell. New York: Auburn House, 1989.

Exploring Early Childhood: Readings in Theory and Practice. M. Kaplan-Sanoff and R. Yablans-Magid, eds. New York: Macmillan, 1981.

Family Day-to-Day Care. Family Day Care Providers. Mt. Ranier, MD: Gryphon House, Inc. $5.95.

Friendly Intruders: Childcare Professionals and Family Life. C.E. Joffe. Berkeley: University of California Press, 1977.

A Guide for Planning and Operating Home-Based Child Development Programs. U.S. Department of Health and Human Services (DHEW Publication No. OHD 75-1080), U.S. Government Printing Office, Washington, D.C.

How to Start a Day Care Center. Day Care Council of America, 711 14th Street, NW, Wash., DC 20005, $5.95.

Inviting Parents into the Young Child's World. K.J. Swick. Champaign, IL: Stipes Co., 1984.

The Joy of Movement in Early Childhood. S.R. Curtis. New York: Teachers College Press, 1982. $12.95.

Mainstreaming Handicapped Students: A Guide for the Classroom Teacher. A. Turnbull and J. Schylz. Boston: Allyn and Bacon, 1979.

Managing the Day Care Dollars: A Financial Handbook. Gryphon House, 3706 Otis Street, P.O. Box 275C., Mt. Rainier, MD 20712. $7.95.

Practical Guide to Solving Preschool Behavior Problems. Eva Essa. Delmar Publishers, Inc.

Promoting the Social Development of Young Children. Strategies and Activities. C.A. Smith, Mayfield Publishing, 285 Hamilton Avenue, Palo Alto, CA 94301.

The Psychosocial Development of Minority Group Children. G.J. Powell, J. Yamamoto, A. Romero, and A. Morales. New York: Brunner/Mazel, 1983. $60.00.

School-Age Child Care; An Action Manual. R.K. Baden, A. Genser, J.A. Levine, and M. Seligson. Boston: Auburn House, 1982. $12.00.

Smart Toys for Babies from Birth to Two. Kent G. Burtt and K. Kalkstein. Cambridge, MA: Harper Colophon, 1981.

Think of Something Quiet: A Guide for Achieving Serenity in Early Childhood Classrooms. C. Cherry. Belmont, CA: Pitman Learning, 1981.

The Toddler Center. M. O'Brien, J. Porterfield, E. Herbert-Jackson, and T.R. Risley. Baltimore: University Park Press, 1979.

Young Children in Action. M. Hohmann, B. Banet, and D. Weikart. Ypsilanti, MI: High/Scope Educational Research Foundation, 1979. $15.00.

Your Baby and Child: From Birth to Age Five. P. Leach. New York: Knopf: 1981. $15.95.

Your Toddler. Richard R. Rubin, John J. Fisher III, and Susan C. Doering. New York: Macmillan, 1980. $9.95.

Index

Index.1

Index.5